MW01383185

INNER CITY LIVING

Radka,

Gonna miss you the most, shh.. don't tell no one! You have such a kindness and selfworth, that is so real, You possess an inner beauty that is very unique, don't ever change! And your are so friggen funny!!

Your friend forever

John Radka

INNER CITY LIVING:

Deviant Behavior

John Hodish Jr.

Copyright © 2011 by John Hodish Jr.

Library of Congress Control Number:		2011907465
ISBN:	Hardcover	978-1-4628-7058-5
	Softcover	978-1-4628-7057-8
	Ebook	978-1-4628-7059-2

All rights reserved. No part of this book may be reproduced or transmitted in any form or by any means, electronic or mechanical, including photocopying, recording, or by any information storage and retrieval system, without permission in writing from the copyright owner.

This book was printed in the United States of America.

To order additional copies of this book, contact:
Xlibris Corporation
1-888-795-4274
www.Xlibris.com
Orders@Xlibris.com
99034

CONTENTS

Author's Dedication

My wife, Ruth Ann, who has been through many painful years with me, who endured my pain as if it were her own, who embraced and loved me for who I am, and who never once tried to change me, I truly love you. To my daughters, Lianne and Madalyn, you two are the fibers of my being; you two brought me much joy and happiness, and I love you always. To Mom and Dad Schulte, you two helped establish an identity for a young troubled man; and without your support and love, this book would never have been written. I love you.

Preface

"Crabs in a barrel is what the inner city really is, John," so says John Major Medlin, my good friend and my referral from a black man's perspective while writing this manuscript. Before I go into what "crabs in a barrel" is referring to, an introduction of both Mr. Medlin and myself is needed. Mr. Medlin was born and raised in the city of Clairton, where most of this manuscript will refer to. He is forty-nine years old, a Muslim, and a Black Panther. For those who do not know what a Black Panther is, this is a member of an organization that promotes the safety and positive growth of the black communities throughout the United States, for the most part. Many feel, and this is pointed to the white community throughout the United States, that the Panthers are an aggressive group that brings terror upon the white society. This is furthest from the truth. Yes, the Panthers were involved in some instances where death and destruction may have occurred; however, if one would research how these instances started, one would find that the Panthers were protecting their own.

Anyway, Mr. Medlin has a perspective very similar to mine, which I guess stems from the fact that we were both exposed to a life of poverty, strife, and the struggle to survive, or at least to get by. What is unique about our relationship, and confuses just about everybody, is that I am white and a Christian of strong faith. Many people, both white and black, can't understand how this can be. Well, I will tell you how this can be. We have the capacity to understand mankind, how cruelty can be imposed on another unjustly. And while we can understand how this came to be, we both understand that it is a gross injustice in the eyes of God or Allah. The inequalities that exist within any inner city has reached past the racial boundaries, and now while many black communities still suffer from racism, prejudices, and biases, the white communities are beginning to understand this much better now that the financial hardships are beginning to affect them as well. Financial depression is the common denominator between the whites and blacks, and to keep it a full stack (street jargon for being honest), financial depression is felt by all races. I am using whites and blacks because these are the races that I live with.

Let us get back to the "crabs in a barrel" and what Mr. Medlin was referring to. Mr. Medlin states that if there was a barrel (such as a rain barrel) with about fifty crabs in it, every time one would try to surface to the top, another crab below the water surface would reach with its clawed limb and clamp on to the crab that is striving to reach the surface and pull it back underwater. The crab that is clamping on to the other crab that is trying to surface really doesn't understand why pulling the other crab down under the water is necessary but, out of instinct perhaps, does so. This, as Mr. Medlin states, is the same scenario happening within the inner city. Every time a resident is trying to break free of this brick-and-mortar prison (the rain barrel), someone always pulls them back in. Why this phenomenon occurs will be explained throughout this manuscript.

Language is another area that Mr. Medlin and I talk about frequently. He views language as a way to appease the black community. An example is the word "nigger" or "neeger." These words, as viewed by the black community, are derogatory of course; but there is a deep-seated, almost ingrained into the African-American community, meaning that lowers the black race to a standard that is less than an animal. This is a response that is understandable, at least from my perspective, and one that could invoke such hostility that could bring one to a state of violence. The cost of life that is associated with these words is staggering. These words today were replaced with the terms "gangs," "thugs," "hoods," and "ghettos." The overseers are the law enforcement officials, and the house niggas are the blacks who run to the white man in hopes of gaining favor. These house niggas snitch on the field niggas who are trying to do their best just to survive and would never concede to the favoring of a white man. Oh yeah, this mentality does exist.

An incident occurred to exemplify this example of language. I will not use the house nigga's name, as Mr. Medlin referred to this individual in front of the mayor, chief of police, and many of the city council members present at a meeting that was provoked by this specific individual, who ran to the city officials to tell on Mr. Medlin and his so-called wrongdoings. As we were sitting at the counsel table discussing the so-called wrongdoings of Mr. Medlin, Mr. Medlin looked at this other black man, the tattletale, and called him a "house nigga." The city officials were shocked, I chuckled, and the so-called house nigga didn't say a word. The meeting broke up very quickly. Mr. Medlin, while an explanation was not necessary because I completely understood what the term "house nigga" implied, felt that he needed to explain. He did, and he also referred to me as being a "field nigger" if I were black and lived during the days of slavery. I accepted being called a field nigger as a compliment, truly.

The truth is being accepted into the black community throughout society is very important to me. Oh, and by the way, the term for this would be a "nigger lover" or "Sammy." Why, you might ask, is being accepted and appreciated by the black community so important? It is because I can truly feel the pain and suffering that this race has endured. Yes, there are other races that endured atrocities similar to those endured by the African-American race, but I wasn't raised with these other races. This does not imply that I don't care; it's just that I can't relate as well. I want the world to know that I am proud to have been able to walk with this community and walk for this community. Ultimately, I hope and pray that all of society will understand that I have the capacity to love and praise and, lastly, call all who live in the inner cities, regardless of race, my brothers and sisters and also any human being, regardless of where they live.

The time has come to forgive but to never forget the tumultuous past. Yes, that means you, my black brothers and sisters. And for you, white people, quit it. It is time to stop all of this childish behavior; and it is time to recognize all as equals, to right the wrongs, and to give where giving is needed.

I am hoping that this manuscript will encourage people to begin a serious soul searching process. I am with hope that many will find this manuscript an aid in understanding and a tool to use, on a professional level, to assist those who really do need counseling and can't afford it. Try as we might, we as human beings will never be perfect. No one will, but as long as we can walk in honesty and try to appreciate the beauty that every unique individual has to offer, this would be a wonderful start.

I will always be ever so thankful to John Major Medlin because forming a friendship with him has been truly enlightening. This friendship has crossed so many boundaries imposed by mankind that it is almost delightful—you know, that giddy feeling one gets when he or she is so ever thankful for a genuine display of positive human emotion? The one thing that inspires me more than anything is the hope that this attempt at providing society with a factual manuscript into the heart of inner-city living will one day proves fruitful. What a legacy that would be!

Another truth that I would like to expose you readers who are attempting to gain insight into a world that is frightful and very much misunderstood is that the gangbangers and deviants (I really do not like to use this word, but keeping with the norms of society, this is almost required to differentiate between good and bad) within the small inner city of Clairton, Pennsylvania, and the residents themselves are the most sincere, loving, proud people I have ever known. To be welcomed into their world with open arms is ever so gratifying. This acceptance speaks volumes in that while many will see this world as tragic and scary, which it is for an outsider, the capacity of the residents within this inner city to love, hope, and care for one another is genuine. I have never met a group of people who have been so genuine . . . And I love you for this.

Abstract

The inner city of Clairton, Pennsylvania, will be analyzed in regard to the deviant behavior that brings about a very high crime rate due to poverty, gangs, drugs and alcohol use, abuse, and/or addiction. This manuscript will suggest that not only are the existing detrimental variables present within the inner city of Clairton, but these same variables are present throughout every inner city within our vast society, the commonality being the group mentality and how this mentality views daily life and the choices offered within the inner cities.

The many inequalities that exist within the inner cities will be exposed within this manuscript. Also, the lack of culture and education has created a loss of self-identity. This will be discussed extensively as this is the key element in the formation of the individual deviant mind-set, which is the foundation of the group mentality. The terrorist (or gang) perspective is the group mentality that is under scrutiny within this suggested perspective of inner-city life. The community in general is suffering from the Stockholm syndrome—accepting the hostage takers' (gangs') perspective or, in the least, turning their eyes from the criminal activity in fear of retaliation.

The CCOP, which has been established over the past three years, has developed an effective way of alleviating deviant behavior within the city of Clairton. The CCOP has received the country's highest award offered, the Allegheny County Proclamation Award, for its efforts in mentoring the young and in alleviating deviant behavior within the city of Clairton. Also, a letter from the mayor and the chief of police was given to the CCOP in recognition of the efforts made to alleviate the deviant behavior within the city of Clairton. The crime rate was reduced significantly in the third year of the CCOP's existence.

The Clairton Community Outreach Program (CCOP) Center.
If viewed closely, the brick is painted blue,
and the window has a bullet hole.

The integrated therapeutic method offered as a way to alleviate the current mentality within the inner cities are the psychodynamic method and the family systems thinking approach. The psychodynamic model, while still holding much of the traditional approach, does offer a new way of delivering this method of recovery. The role of the counselor and client in this new approach of the therapeutic process of the psychodynamic model is one that could be described as a mild collaboration, whereas the counselor must always remain in control of the therapeutic process. The psychodynamic approach will be used as the initial assessment tool to determine the process of recovery and the alternatives that are present for the client. Once the assessment of the client is finalized, introducing the client to the next stage of recovery will be made, the CCOP's family system thinking process.

The family system thinking model also holds the same tradition values; but again, certain modifications have been made within the CCOP because of the clientele, gangbangers and the community as a whole, or the majority of the community, which this manuscript suggests is suffering from Stockholm syndrome. The modifications concern the counselor's or therapist's roles and posture, specifically when dealing with adolescents. Specific interventions are also introduced as are the limitations that are present with the CCOP's version of the family systems thinking model.

The conclusion will bind the history of the inner cities and the therapeutic process that will alleviate deviance throughout our society. The importance of formulating a process of recovery that is geared not only on an individual perspective but also on the group mentality is necessary to alleviate the deviance within the inner cities.

As can be seen, the Crips spray-painted (tagged) 187 on this building. This means a homicide will occur.

Acknowledgments

First and foremost, I would like to say that God has blessed me in so many ways. He has provided me with many skills to spread his kingdom; and with this, all the glory goes to my savior, Jesus Christ. My beautiful wife, Ruth Ann, who has recognized my compassion for those who live within the inner cities throughout our society, an extra I love you goes out to her. If not for my wife, I would be dead or in prison. She has spent many hours alone and sacrificed much for the purpose of letting me find myself in this manuscript that has been written. My two daughters—Lianne and Madalyn. Lianne, who is the older, has always brought much joy into my life and has demonstrated her sincerity of love in so many ways that I cannot even begin to explain. My younger daughter, Madalyn, has an ability to make people laugh and has a passion for life that is truly inspirational. She made some bad times good. My family is all that I live for. I am truly devoted to these girls. They have provided me warmth and comfort that I pray all could experience. I will always love you, ladies, forever. You three girls are the fiber of my being.

My mother-in-law and father in-law. If not for them, my educational journey would never have been possible. These are the two most beautiful people whom I have ever known. Their kindness, warmth, and understanding are uniquely strong. I have so much to thank them for that a book could be written with all of their generous, unselfish acts that they have bestowed upon me. Their extended love to a boy, who would be me, from the other side of the tracks has affected me profoundly in so many positive ways. This demonstration of love for another is remarkable, and I am ever so grateful to them for so many reasons. Mom and Dad, I love you both with every fiber of my being.

I want to extend a special thank-you to three individuals who have helped me tremendously in my endeavor to expose the truths about inner-city life. John Major Medlin, who is from the same inner city as I am, has been nothing less than a true friend. John, or Philly as he is known throughout the community, has endured many hours of my babbling about personal issues, conflicts of interest within the outreach program, and, at times, just memories of a lifetime that seems so long ago. He and I share a common history, growing up in a time of such racism, prejudices, and hatred. We have come to know one truth—that ignorance is no excuse for condemnations. The uniqueness of our friendship has many people baffled because I am white and he is black. I am Christian, and he is Muslim and a member of the Black Panthers. And we are bound by a certain spirituality that only the luckiest will ever experience. He is my true friend, and I love him. Not only has Philly been a true friend of mine, but he was a huge resource in providing me much insight into the black community.

Tristan Geletko is another true friend who has provided me many years of devotion and loyalty that can only come from an individual who is filled with passion and love for all mankind. While Tristan displays certain ruggedness being a man's man, he truly is one of the kindest and gentlest men I have ever known. His commitment to family and friends has provided me strength and resolve in that there is good in all mankind, if you looked hard enough. I love you, Aleata, and the children with all of my heart.

Dr. Kimberly Maring, a Christian woman, had taken a liking to me while teaching one of my classes in my undergraduate program. She did much to encourage my writings, and she extended a service through helping with editing this manuscript, which aided so much in the finalization of this endeavor. I love her for her compassion and devotion. And although we have never met, I feel as though I have known her for a lifetime. She is my spiritual sister, and I admire her so much.

And lastly, to all you inner-city dwellers, I love you all; and I will always be available to you forever. Your strength and determination and your compassion for life that only the downtrodden will ever experience are the true reasons for my success. I have learned much in the trenches of the inner city. I have found God in these trenches, and I have overcome much because of the inner city. The truth is if not for the inner city, I would not be the man that I am today. I love you all.

Research Design

In this book, the history and effect of young male deviance in inner-city America will be explored. The naturalistic approach without intervention and the observation with intervention method was and still is being used in this research endeavor and will be explained within this manuscript. The conclusions of the author concerning the cultural ability to change young male deviance within the inner city will also be presented.

The experimental method chosen in the study of deviance within the inner city was the naturalistic approach without intervention. The naturalistic approach without intervention can be defined as "direct observation of behavior in a natural setting, without any attempt by the observer to intervene" (Zechmeister, Zechmeister, and Shaughnessy 2001, 85). However, throughout this study, there were times when the opportunity was afforded to use the observation with intervention method, specifically structured observation, which could be defined as "when the observer intervenes in order to cause an event to occur or to set up a situation so that events can be more easily recorded" (Zechmeister et al. 2001, 85). The latter was used frequently at the Clairton Boxing Club, a community outreach program that focuses on helping troubled adolescents. The staff at the community outreach program was afforded this opportunity of study because of the public outcry of demanding programs such as this to help educate the adolescents of the city of Clairton. An example of one of the structured observation studies performed was to decorate the facility with quotes from the Bible written on the walls and hanging posters of famous African-Americans. This brought about a sense of pride, and the vast majority of African-American males were readily available for discussion pertaining to the famous figures or Bible quotes that were displayed. The premise was that role modeling was needed to help alter the perceptions of the vast majority of African-American males who came through our doors.

This subculture that exists throughout the United States—that is, inner-city dwellers, or those whose lives are subjected to the inner city—is one that is purely territorial. Without the proper credentials, such as police officers or any court-ordered personnel, entering these areas can be very dangerous for people who are not known in the community, hence the reason for the chosen methods of study. To receive a pure and valid conclusion to this ongoing study, trying to manipulate the variables pertaining to internal validity could not apply. Causing any kind of changes within this environment or study would invalidate the question asked in this study: why does deviant behavior within inner cities exist at the level that it does?

Fortunately, I was given a pass, so to speak, to enter some of these inner cities because I was born and raised in an area such as this. It gave the exposure I needed to be recognized throughout my community; and the reputation that I have acquired throughout my community has helped, being a tough, loving, and caring individual.

The sampling plan of this study was primarily any African-American male or Caucasian male who happened to be living within the inner city of Clairton. Although this study is based primarily on African-American males, Caucasian males born and raised within the inner city, although a smaller population, were found to be similarly deviant. Females of the said races were also observed. However, their role within the inner city is much different from those that this research intended to study.

The ethical concerns of this study were few. However, the moral fiber of the observer was questioned at times. Because of the research being a naturalistic approach, this study observed the behaviors of the deviants within an inner city. While there were many incidents that occurred, these incidents would have occurred regardless of whether this study was in effect or not. There were times when crimes could have been stopped by the observer, or at the least, these crimes could have been reported and were not done so immediately. The crimes that were witnessed were reported after the fact, and while some minor crimes—such as petty theft, verbal assaults, or an occasional drug deal—happened, life was never threatened.

The ethical violations, such as those just reported, were of great concern; however, the validity of this study outweighed the crimes that were witnessed. If these particular variables were manipulated in any way, the essence of this study would have been violated, and the integrity of this observer would have been tainted; the criminal/deviant behavior would have ceased when this observer was present.

The expected results of this study pertaining to the high percentage of crime within the inner city, specifically black on black crime, have already been found. The U.S. Census Bureau can confirm these findings, being that the relevant statistical facts are publicly available, and these findings are outside of the scope of this study. This study was pursued to find the measures needed to reduce deviant behavior within the inner cities and to offer the needed course of action to alter the perceptions of those within the inner city of Clairton.

The question that is intriguing with the study of deviant behavior within the inner city would be the question of external validity, which is defined as "a research study or experiment has external validity if the results obtained would apply to other similar programs or approaches" (Ender 1998). This study and the conclusions that were obtained would work in any environment; the modification of certain variables would have to be altered to fit the situation. However, the approach would be the same. If we were to relocate this study to the suburbs or rural areas, the same method of observation would apply, as would any and all of the ethical and moral concerns. Since this study is concerned primarily with black-on-black crimes and how these activities are spilling over into the suburbs, the conclusion would be different, but the alteration of perceptions would remain the same.

The limitations pertaining specifically to the conclusions of this study have not yet been found; the limitations of this study would be significant in that these limitations would unjustly damage any findings that have been found by using the methods that were and are yet to come. This is an extraordinary study into a major concern of deviant behavior, and the growth of this behavior will continue unless changes can be made. These changes have to be on a personal level, which will be very costly. However, in order to tame this beast, deviant behavior within the inner city, the cost and effort made by all have to be made.

This study is not to condemn, raise speculation, or discriminate against any race. This document is to suggest that deviant behavior has and always will exist and to give insight as to why the level of black-on-black crime has skyrocketed.

With little evidence to support the psychological or biological theories of deviant behavior, the sociological aspect of deviant behavior stands in the forefront pertaining to a valid explanation as to what deviant behavior is and how deviant behavior is manifested. Sutherland and Vechten (1934) demonstrate, in reference to the differential association theory, that "[c]riminal behavior is learnable and learned in interaction with other deviant persons. Through this association, they learn not only techniques of certain crimes, but also specific rationale, motives and so on. These associations vary in frequency, duration, etc. Differential association theory explains why any individual forwards toward deviant behavior. His assertion is most useful when explaining peer influences among deviant youths or special mechanism of becoming certain criminal."

Perspective of Deviant Behavior within the Inner City

The perspective of deviant behavior is shared by all: the rich, poor, two-parent households, single-parent households, etc. Being that the perception of deviance will vary in our society and what some in our society will deem acceptable behavior, an invisible line has been drawn separating the norms and deviant behavior. This is what poses the question as to what deviant behavior is and whether this behavior is acceptable or not.

The arrival of Africans to Jamestown was due to a Dutch slave trader who exchanged his cargo of Africans for food in 1619. The chains of slavery exist to this day, in other forms—the inner cities. As stated by Donald (1971), "The first twenty 'Negar' slaves had arrived from the West Indies in a Dutch vessel, were sold to the governor and a merchant in Jamestown in late August of 1619, as reported by John Rolfe to John Smith back in London." This date can be said to be the beginning of the slave trade within the United States.

Ghettos, slums, the inner city—this is the promised land of freedom given to our African-American brothers and sisters in retribution for condemning this race to slavery. Within the confines of this brick-and-mortar prison, the projects, the ghettos, and the slums, crime has always been and still is. We, white America and even some African-Americans, have created a monster that may not be tamed for quite some time. We offered freedom and gave them this, a place to reside that offers despair, hate, solitude from the educational world, welfare to provide minimally to the families of the inner city, drugs, and alcohol to spread crime.

The acknowledgment of our deeds has to be recognized. We need to own up to what we have created, and to do this will take more than a simple apology. This will take an ongoing effort to educate in order to reinstate trust, loyalty, and compassion within the inner cities.

Observing the crime that is occurring is naturally the first stage of this study. Crime within the inner cities and how this attitude/perspective is branching out into all of society are also of great concern. Deviant behavior, a definition will soon follow, has been in existence forever; and this deviance will continue. However, we can alter the level of deviance within the inner cities. Let us start by examining the confines of the inner city. What we have is a community that lives in proximity to each other; families are afforded very little privacy. This closeness offers a spirited allegiance, a social phenomenon, an allegiance to a specific group. This territorial aggression is brought about by the depressed areas in which they live. They, meaning gangs or cliques, protect their turf so as to protect their financial gain on the streets. So protecting the neighborhood by any and all costs is exactly what happens. Many sell drugs, use drugs, prostitute, and murder just to get by; they do whatever is necessary to pay the bills and support their families.

The starting point of reference the author will use to demonstrate the racism and prejudice suffered by the African-Americans will be May 17, 1954. This is the day that the "United States Supreme Court rules in Brown vs. Board of Education of Topeka, Kansas, that racial segregation in the public schools is inherently unequal and, therefore, illegal" (Brown Foundation for Educational Equity 2004). This event was just fifty-five years ago, and while this ruling was in effect, racism and prejudice still exist to this day. To further this timeline of injustices directed toward the African-Americans, we can date back to "September 15, 1963 when four children died when the church they were attending was bombed in Birmingham" (White 2000).

Being that this struggle for equality existed for so long and, in many cases, still does exist, the attitude that African-Americans should "forgive and forget" is an attitude held by many Caucasians in this country. However, seeing one's family members brutalized physically and mentally is an event that would take longer than a mere fifty-five years.

What this study is suggesting is that this destructive behavior of the inner city dwellers is learned, a response directed toward those whom they feel warrants this behavior. Anyone who tries to take what they feel belongs to them. This could be the drug trade, their territory pertaining to anything that can threaten these inner-city dwellers as far as financial gain or any territorial issue that may arise, or when these inhabitants feel threatened by them.

The migration of African-Americans into the inner city was due in most part to job opportunities and racism. The affordable living quarters that the inner city offered was the first opportunity at this time to get away from racism and to seek gainful employment. When this migration occurred, the Caucasians moved into the suburbs to avoid living within a black community, creating a racial barrier that exists to this day.

In the year of 1954, the Supreme Court made the decision to strike down racial segregation in public schools. In the year of 1957, Little Rock, Arkansas, began this desegregation process. This state began racial integration throughout the state. The public busing, libraries, zoos, and park systems were finally opened up to the African-American community. However, this attempt did not go without incident. On September 2, 1957, Arkansas governor Orval Faubus called out the National Guard in order to prevent the African-American students from entering the school. Governor Orval Faubus did this to prevent any uncivil acts that may occur due to this attempt of integration. This movement carried on until September 23, 1957, and was then over turned by a federal judge who "granted an injunction against the Governor's use of National Guard troops to prevent integration and they were withdrawn on September 20" (Rains 2000). While we may mark this event as being significant in the equality of all, we can also mark this date as being the most recent attempt for equality. The struggle for equality still exists, and this document will hopefully trigger a response noting that the struggle for equality is still going on.

Explanation of Deviant Behavior

If deviant behavior is to be viewed as an act outside of the norms of society (e.g., murder, car theft, or just telling a white lie), then to explain deviant behavior, we would have to justify societal views as a whole; however, some view telling a small mistruth as acceptable as long as no harm has come from this little white lie. In understanding the different levels of deviant behavior, we as a society must appreciate the acceptable norms in the subcultures of any society. While the majority of society will see deviant behavior as outside the norms of our culture, if we were to examine the norms of deviance within a subculture (for example, the Bloods street gang), this deviant behavior is acceptable in that particular subculture. This is a way of life; these are acts of survival. The Bloods and many street gangs have the perspective that they are not much different from Robin Hood, stealing from the rich and giving back to the poor. From an interactionist perspective, "interactionist" being defined as the study of human group life and conduct, Herbert Blumer (1969) stated:

> [H]umans are pragmatic actors who continually must adjust their behavior to the actions of other actors. We can adjust to these actions only because we are able to interpret them, i.e., to denote them symbolically and treat the actions and those who perform them as symbolic objects. This process of adjustment is aided by our ability to imaginatively rehearse alternative lines of action before we act. (Herbert Blumer's *Symbolic Interactionism*)

The connection that we as a society value is that normal behavior, or social bonds, that keep a society aligned with the institutions that govern deviant behavior has been the fiber of our society, being that our perspectives are similar when discussing deviant behavior helps us to differentiate between good and bad behavior. The control theory "asserts that normal behavior is shaped by the power of social control mechanisms in our culture. Put differently, the social bonds that connect people help to keep us from committing deviance" (Glasser 1985).

If we were to examine the control theory closer, we would identify certain characteristics that would constitute our social bonds. As Glasser (1985) states in his control theory, there are six commonalities that we all strive for, these six being the following: survival, power, love, belonging, freedom, and fun. While this may stand true, Glasser's ten axioms of choice is argumentative, at least the first two, which state:

1. The only person whose behavior we can control is our own.
2. All we can give another person is information.

In Glasser's first axiom, the only person whose behavior we can control is our own. This statement is misleading. While we cannot control one's actions, we can certainly control one's behavior, as is supported by this entire document. Behavior modification can be controlled, and behavior can be altered. However, the environment needs to be changed of the individual whose behavior needs to be modified.

Secondly, in Glasser's second axiom, he states that all we can give another person is information. This is argumentative in that our emotional state can be shared, which in most cases will be reflected through the individual receiving this particular emotion. For instance, showing and demonstrating affection can be received by another and usually will be reciprocated in the same manner by the other person.

Viewing the vast society in which we live, the United States, our society has formed a societal attachment. This would be how the vast majority of a society connects. First, let us look at Bowlby's theory of attachment. According to Bowlby (1953):

> [W]e as infants seek the parental bond for many reasons. The assumption being that we as infants respond accordingly to our needs, such as when we are hungry we cry out, when we are in pain, we cry out, and when we seek comfort we also cry out, etc. How the caretaker responds to the needs of the infant will relate to how the infants behavior will develop. If the child's needs are ignored, and the caretaker is fundamentally inept at caregiving, the behavioral growth of the child will be affected negatively.

This is not to say that the child as an adult will be at a higher level of deviant behavior, which is possible, but the child as an adult will suffer in building meaningful relationships.

What is being offered in this document, and building off Bowlby's theory of attachment is that while Bowlby's theory is valid, how we should approach those who are suffering from a void of attachment as an infant and through his or her adolescent stages of development could suggest the desire or need of acceptance, which, in the inner cities, would be the inclusion into a gang. According to Rutter M. (1979) in his book ***Maternal Deprivation***, "The underlying assumption of Bowlby's Maternal Deprivation Hypothesis is that continual disruption of the attachment between infant and primary caregiver (i.e. mother) could result in long term cognitive, social, and emotional difficulties for that infant" (pp. 283-305). To further the detrimental growth pattern of a child who may have been exposed to maternal deprivation, as stated by S. A. McLeod (2007), "the long-term consequences of maternal deprivation might include the following: delinquency, reduced intelligence, increased aggression, depression, affectionless psychopathy." McLeod (2007)also states, "Affectionless psychopathy is an inability show affection or concern for others. Such of individuals act on impulse with little regard for the consequences of their actions. For example, showing no guilt for antisocial behaviour" (p. 14).

Inner-City Morality

In inner-city deviance, "charisma" and "swagger" are words to describe a sought-after persona to identify leadership or one being the "king of the hill," so to speak. The deviant charisma is one based on how successful one can be at operating outside the norms of society, and with certain "swagger," an image of self-assuredness will emerge. Swagger, defined as self-assuredness, is common to the vast majority of deviants, whether the criminal activity is white-collar or juvenile deviance, although this swagger is more noticeable in juvenile deviance. Juvenile deviance and the level at which we would gauge a specific act outside of the norms of society can be observed by the fear factor that a certain player projects, and usually, this fear factor can offer insight at the level of deviance this player is capable of. For example, a commonality that convicts display in their appearance is teardrops tattooed on their face right by the corner of their eye; the number of tattoos indicates how many lives they have taken. The common street gang member is seen in the Jets (this is a street term used for projects, an apartment complex for low-income families) and wears saggy jeans, a football jersey, a gold grill (this is a fitted dental plate that covers teeth), earrings, tattoos—these are indicators that this could be a possible deviant player. The loudness—not only verbal, but the style and swagger that an individual has—is also an indicator that this person could be a menace to our society. This could be taken as stereotyping. It is a cultural norm of dress in the inner city that is recognized by that culture; and to confront an individual who is dressed liked this, one should be extremely careful, depending on where a confrontation occurs.

Another approach used to explain deviance is the Cloward and Ohlin's strain theory (1960). To recapitulate their hypothesis, "the disparity between what lower-class youth are led to want and what is actually available to them is the source of a major problem of adjustment" (Cloward and Ohlin 1960, 86). Although this does not explain white-collar deviance, this theory does offer a plausible explanation as to why lower-class youth can become deviant. As witnessed at Auberle, a placement shelter for deviant adolescents, and depending on whether or not their psychological diagnosis found the individual to be suffering from a mental disorder, all the residents who were not suffering from mental disorders explained that they have no problem taking from others or doing what is necessary to achieve a certain street status and that the valuables that they have taken will be turned over into another means to produce more money, such as buying and selling "street drugs."

Another theory that explains deviance and which is very similar to Cloward and Ohlin's strain theory (1960) would be Merton's theory of anomie (Merton 1940). In Merton's formulation, "anomie becomes the explanation for high rates of deviant behavior in the U.S. compared with other societies, and also an explanation for the distribution of deviant behavior across groups defined by class, race, ethnicity, and the like" (Merton 1940). This could explain why deviant behavior exists; however, one may argue that deviant behavior exists not only in poverty-stricken communities but in any walk of life. And while this argument may be statistically valid, the needs of an individual may not necessarily be monetary. There are many needs that we as individuals strive for besides monetary items, such as power among peers, love, greed, and envy; and while Merton's theory of anomie may be suggestive of monetary gain, this theory could be expanded upon in these needs also. When the means to justify the gains of any individual who are trying to achieve a desirable goal is not present, some individuals will do what they feel is necessary to achieve this goal; and when a legitimate means is nonexistent, deviant behavior may occur. For this reason, according to Merton, "deviance is the result of an almost universal cultural desire for material security, success, and comfort on one hand, and limited opportunities to achieve these things on the other hand" (Petee 1987).

Deviance is universal, and the different levels of deviance are where most of the confusion begins. Being a counselor at a nearby placement shelter for deviants and those who suffer from mental illness, I know there have been many opportunities to test these theories of deviance, and the conclusion that I have witnessed after interviewing over two hundred adolescent young men and women has been that they need positive peer acceptance. They come from poor family relationships, single-parent households, drug and alcohol abuse, and a lack of education, which when combined will set a path of serious deviant behavior. Recently, an endeavor is being made to ascertain the seriousness of deviant behavior when combinations of the said indicators are minus one or more of the detriments stated above. For instance, if an adolescent was not using drugs or alcohol, would his or her behavior be less deviant? If the adolescent came from a household where both parents were present and the use of drugs and alcohol were not present, would the level of deviance be less?

The perspectives of society as well as individual perspectives vary, and societal views on deviance are stigmatized by labeling. Societal views on labeling have been a heated topic because the "strong images are associated with diagnostic labels and people act upon these images. Sometimes the images are useful generalizations; sometimes they are harmful stereotypes. Sometimes they guide practitioners toward good ways to help; sometimes they contribute to 'blaming the victim,' making young people the focus of intervention rather than pursuing system deficiencies that are causing the problem in the first place. In all cases, diagnostic labels can profoundly shape a person's future" (School Mental Health Project, UCLA).

We as a society have to be mindful of the differences pertaining to cultural morality. Because the inner cities need to create ownership of their particular neighborhoods and because of the immense differences in the norms of the inner-city culture as opposed to those outside of this brick-and-mortar reservation, morality differences are vast. A nonfictional example follows:

This is a nonfictional event about a young man in my community who attended my amateur boxing club. His name will be changed. James was five years old when he witnessed his uncle being murdered by his father, stabbed to death in his apartment where he lived with his mother. James came to my program center when he was nine years old. He showed a lot of potential in this sport of boxing, and all he did was smile. I did not know the history of James at this time, short period of just a few weeks, until I got a phone call from the chief of police stating that he would like me and Reverend Stoudemire to go to James's home. There was a domestic dispute between James and his mother; I found out en route of the murder incident. When we got to the home, James was in tears, as was his mother. James threw the Christmas presents out of the second-floor window because he was not allowed to open one present on Christmas Eve. James confirmed this. We explained to James that respecting his mother was very important, and he replied how he can do this when all his mother does all day was smoke crack. Since this incident occurred, James has been in and out of placement shelters twice. He is currently at his third placement shelter.

I realize that this goes beyond just a moral dilemma, but a moral dilemma does exist, and this is what my focus is on. James has been going through life juggling the issue of right and wrong, especially since his father was released because of the claim that this act of taking another's life was in self-defense, and I am not sure of the intricacies of the case. However, I do believe that this act of murder distorted James's moral judgment. Wilson (1993) states, "Consequently, if we were to live with one another—if society is to be possible—we must share certain conceptions of what is right and what is wrong" (p. 308). This is where I think James's confusion began. And to compound this dilemma, watching his mother do drugs did not help.

After studying both Piaget's and Kohlberg's theories of moral development, I found that Piaget's theory of moral development seemed to fit. I do see a correlation between James's lack of moral development and what Piaget describes in his heteronomous morality stage. Piaget (1932) states in the first stage of his two-stage theory, the heteronomous morality stage, that "children are immersed in an authoritarian environment in which they occupy a position decidedly inferior to that of adults, and in this context children develop a conception of moral rules as absolute, unchanging, and rigid" (p. 310).

This is where James's dilemma began. He knew that what he witnessed was wrong, but the court system found his father innocent. And even if he was, murder was wrong. And maybe what he witnessed was in fact murder and was not in self-defense; and if this were the case, James's moral development would surely be affected.

In Piaget's (1932) second stage of moral development, the autonomous stage, Piaget states that "morality evolves from the unequal relationships between children and adults; autonomous morality arises from the interaction among status equals-relationships amongst peers" (p. 310). Being that James lives in a community where acts of violence like gangbanging are acceptable furthers the positive moral development in any child, especially after this particular child, James, witnessed a murder. This almost solidifies the belief that in some cases, murder can be acceptable.

As far as Kohlberg's stages of moral development is concerned, every stage of development could be applied. I would have to disagree in his belief of universal moral development. Justice and equality do not exist in every environment.

If we were to break down Erikson's stages of development and apply them to the inner-city youth, the stages would look like this, as designed by John Hodish:

INFANT: MISTRUST

Environmental issues play a huge factor at this stage. Even if the parent/parents are raising this child accordingly, most parents know of the negative environmental factors that are present and have a tendency to be restrictive. An imbalance will occur.

TODDLER: SHAME AND DOUBT

Autonomy will never occur, for many, because of the restrictive nature of the family environment. The balance between autonomy versus shame and doubt will never occur. Again, this is, in most, part of the environmental issue. Also, the physical environment, even within the home of the child, is less than appropriate. I have known many loving and caring parents in my community, but being financially depressed and with the educational differences that exist among the inner cities and those school districts that are thriving financially, the means to advance up the social ladder is slim and none.

THE ADDED STAGE: ADJUSTMENT VERSUS MALADJUSTMENT: AGES FOUR TO SIX

The adjustment versus maladjustment stage is meant for intervention. Children in this age-group have a distorted view of reality, and with a child being raised in an environment that is unhealthy both mentally and physically, maladjustment could occur. Children who live in the inner city are at a disadvantage at this stage because of many variables, such as single parenting, living quarters being very close together, lack of positive male role models, and peer pressure. Without intervention at this stage, deviant behavior is probable. Piaget's (1920) sources of continuity could be applied at this stage, which are as follows:

1. Assimilation: People translate incoming information into a form they can understand.
2. Accommodation: People adapt current knowledge structures in response to new experience.
3. Equilibration: People balance assimilation and accommodation to create stable understanding.

(Piaget's Theory: Continuous versus Discontinuous)

Applying assimilation to the inner-city child at this stage of development, when a child is raised in an environment that is filled with negative experiences, the child will accept this behavior as the norm. Being that the child was raised as such his or her entire life, this is all the child knows. This adjustment could lead to deviant behavior if intervention is not afforded, which it is not within the inner cities.

Using accommodation at this stage is vital in the positive growth of the child. Reeducating the child to shift the child's perception of all of the negative experiences and creating positive life-defining moments could enhance the chances of eliminating deviance.

Equilibration could be advantageous; however, this, depending on an individual basis, may be a hindrance to the positive growth of the child. Trying to eliminate the negative input is essential, but remembering the negatives could encourage the child to grow from the negativity. Or this remembrance could trigger a response that the child may have that was actually rewarding, and a relapse may occur.

Once the child navigates through this stage successfully, he or she will then move forward with the opportunity to establish a positive sense of self and will enter the adolescent stage of development. From this point on, the child will be able to enter each stage of development appropriately.

We as a society need to alter our views on deviance, specifically labeling, because this will lead to negative self-image of an individual. Not only does the image of deviant behavior need to be altered, but we as a society need to rethink the fundamental needs of our children in an attempt to subdue deviance.

The Community Resilience Theory

According to John Hodish, the attachment theory in the adolescent stage has to be developed as a community effort. The community resilience theory by John Hodish speculates that assuming that the level of attachment that an adolescent is suffering from within the inner city is void, we as a community have to extend ourselves to thwart this deviant behavior that is being demonstrated by the behavior of the adolescent. The logic of the author is this: if we as a community can modify the destructive behavior of the inner-city youth, we have to extend ourselves into the community. For example, the CCOP has successfully secured a three-block radius where no deviant behavior exists. We do this by patrolling our area with volunteers—a group of adults ranging in age from twenty-one to sixty-five. We approach any individual who enters this three-block radius and offer ourselves as being loving and caring. We are not confrontational; we are polite and nurturing. We speak to these individuals about God and community peace and explain why we are patrolling as we are—to eliminate deviant behavior. We have come to be recognized by the green vests and hats that we wear. We also are coordinated with the city's police. Currently, we are approaching the city churches, asking them to extend themselves in the same way; we have eight churches in the city of Clairton. We have approached the educational system also and have been granted the opportunity to walk the halls of the educational center and been given permission to approach certain adolescents who are having behavioral issues. When we approach those adolescents who are having behavioral issues, we offer them mentorship, we offer them love and passion, we offer them hope and a safe haven from the streets. We are hoping that the churches and the community as a whole will extend themselves as well, and our premise is that if all would become involved, we could then extend ourselves not just three blocks, but an overwhelming fifty or so blocks. It takes a village to raise a child. This is our new motto. At this point, the adolescents, and in some cases adults as well who are demonstrating deviant behavior, will be squeezed back into the shadows, and them finally being the minority, we can reach into these shadows and offer them salvation.

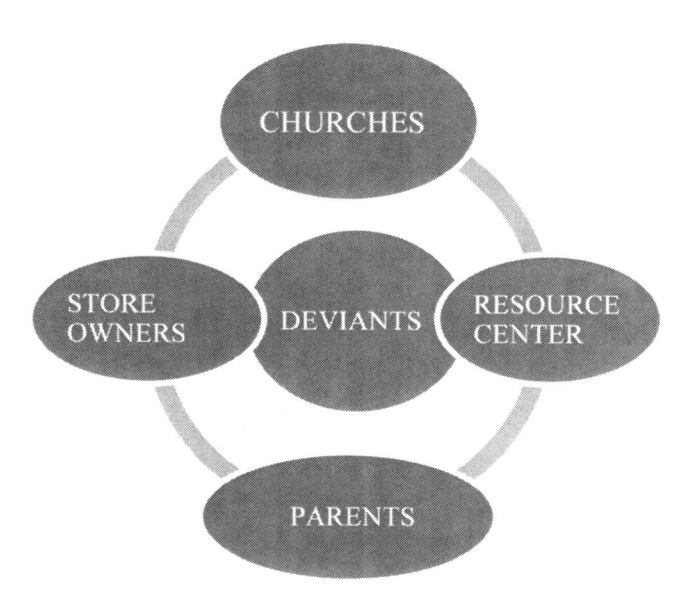

Community Resilience Theory by John Hodish

Allowing our adolescents the freedom to move throughout the community safely is now in place, and with this freedom, the exploration to develop positive defining moments will be possible. Also, this will allow community to reestablish their own community without being dictated by the criminal behavior that is restricting us from personal growth. This community effort is possible, and while this may take three to five years to develop, the effort to educate and treat those who may be suffering from mental and behavioral disorders can be ongoing.

We could say that our freedoms and liberties are bonds that we all share. And with this bond, the laws and institutes that establish certain laws are the tradeoff for our freedoms and liberties; we have to maintain our boundaries as far as being law-abiding citizens is concerned if we are to expect our freedoms and liberties. A commitment toward our communities would also be part of the fiber that bonds us together as a law-abiding society. Having a level of commitment to ensure a peaceful and friendly community is a very important aspect of the control theory. This commitment would extend an individual into the community as an example of a good person—one who abides by the laws set forth and one who genuinely cares for the citizens of one's community. Being involved in community functions is another example that strengthens the bond between an individual and his or her community. Extending ourselves to better our community such as joining the PTA or providing support for the local municipality would be a positive involvement. And lastly, having a strong belief in our community and the citizens who reside there would help in the appearance of a nondeviant individual.

The phenomenon of street gangs is the relational value of each gang member toward what many gang members consider family—the group mentality. This specific journal, *A Systemic Analysis Is of the Dynamics and Organization of Urban Street Gangs,* written by Nikki M. Ruble and William L. Turner (2000), provides the clinical implications of the utility of systems concepts. The key points in this journal are, and as stated by Nikki M. Ruble, William L. Turner (2000):

1. Family systems thinking explains not only why but also how gangs function as a whole.
2. Understanding gangs as systems helps to explain the function that they serve for their members based on a holistic perspective.
3. Systems thinking enables outsiders to understand the structure and hierarchy of gang organization.
4. Knowledge of street gangs from a system's perspective provides information on how members can replace dysfunctional systems with more appropriate, working systems.
5. Understanding the systemic cohesion involved in gang membership provides knowledge about how gangs operate as "family systems."

[A]pplying these systemic concepts to street gangs allows for an acknowledgment that gangs, as all systems, have multiple and complex levels. All levels of street gangs must be reviewed before prevention and intervention strategies will be effective. Viewing gangs from this holistic and systemic perspective provides a number of benefits for both researchers and practitioners. (Ruble and Turner 2000)

This particular article does not demonstrate, statistically, the effectiveness of applying a family systems approach or applying family therapy to this subculture. This article does provide the rationale behind why this approach would be conducive toward understanding and applying certain interventions to alleviate certain hostilities of gang activities and provides a framework as to how to prevent the growth of gangs, to reduce the membership of gangs, and to stop the recruitment of gang members.

*Personal note: The author of this document has spent the last eighteen years researching the inner-city group mentality pertaining to gangs and the acceptance of this activity by the majority of the residents.

Mr. Hodish also provides community outreach within this inner city, which was at one time considered to be the heroin capital of the world. This small inner city has seen gangs such as the Jamaican Boys, Detroit Boys, the Crips, Bloods, and, most recently, the ABM (All Bout Money, a vicious gang that spoke with Mr. Hodish, stating that they will kill anyone who stands against them, including innocent bystanders. They did. This gang was responsible for four murders during the summer of 2009). Over the past three years, the city of Clairton has had a significant decline in crime; and so far this year, there has been only one murder rumored to be gang related.

The, CCOP, which was started in the year of 2007, received the Allegheny County Proclamation Award in recognition of their involvement with the residents of Clairton, specifically the youth, gangbangers. This organization has also received letters of recognition from the chief of police and the mayor of Clairton.

This all was mentioned to provide support to the journal under review—*A Systemic Analysis Is of the Dynamics and Organization of Urban Street Gangs* by Nikki M. Ruble and William L. Turner (2000). Being that the CCOP has received this award and was recognized both from the police and the mayor, the statistics in the decline of criminal behavior, this significant reduction, indicates that the family systems thinking, or systems concept, does work in this type of environment.

The CCOP experiments with many different schools of thought, both on an individual level as well as the group mentality.

Trying to provide any type of realistic statistics is near impossible in this type of environment mostly because of the dangers that exist within a gang infested environment. The author of this document was given a pass so to speak, in this neighborhood, as were his wife and two daughters because he was born and raised here, and has the reputation of being tough, while loving and compassionate. He is known throughout this community.

To briefly speak of some intervention techniques used in the family systems thinking and/or the systemic analysis approach, and according to Ruble and Turner (2000), "if clinicians and researchers understood the systemic functioning of street gangs, interventions could be organized to address all aspects and dimensions of the life of a gang member." Also stated by Ruble and Turner (2000):

> [P]rograms and interventions aimed toward gang members should encompass a multilevel approach, inclusive of individual, family, community, and cultural influences. That understanding power balances and cliques within the gang can be helpful when implementing intervention plans.

Intervention programs that teach gang members job skills and provide job placement will redirect gang members into more positive activities, instead of just lecturing to members that they should not participate in negative gang activities.

First and foremost, in disagreement with this approach is that many times the inclusion of family members is ideally a very good aim; however, through experience at the CCOP, many family members will not participate, in most part, for fear of being recognized as being a family in need, meaning, that their admission to having a problem within this household would be not conducive toward their image of self-worth or the gang affiliation would frown down on this. Also, many inner cities do not have after-school programs, and those that do, do not have the personal to handle this type of clientele.

This article did not speak of specific interventions. However, what has been effective and aligns with the multigenerational family therapy approach, according to the research done at the CCOP, is that, and according to Murray Bowen (1978), "is the notion of differentiation of the self, which involves the psychological separation of intellect and emotion and the independence of self from the others."

Interventions that have been found to be effective at the CCOP are the staff that is used. We use individuals, ex-cons who have been released but still have a parole officer whom he or she answers to, who have a genuine compassion for this type of client and will follow specific guidelines as to what are mission is. Being able to relate to the inner-city population who are suffering from the varied deviant behaviors, using individuals who have been there and done that.

Before we move on, the greatest concern within the inner cities is drug—and alcohol-related disorders and the criminal activity that are associated with the use, abuse, distribution, and addictions of drugs and alcohol. We, the CCOP, have developed guidelines and treatment modalities pertaining to this phenomenon. This section is part of the community resilience program that was created to manage the effects of drugs and alcohol within the inner city.

The CCOP is a community based, pioneering, advanced nongovernment organization that works with individuals, families, groups, communities, and organizations to address alcohol and other drug (AOD) issues in Clairton, Pennsylvania. We build character and strength, and we do this through a rigid program that is focused on health and wellness. Activities that are used to achieve the desired goals of our outreach program are currently amateur or professional boxing and amateur or professional Mixed Martial Arts (MMA). We propose to the local municipalities to court-order any individual, female or male, between the ages of eight and twenty-eight, who may be in danger of serving time within a prison system or placement shelter, to our facility for a period of no less than three months and no longer than one year to help aid in their recovery.

THE CLAIRTON COMMUNITY OUTREACH PROGRAM (CCOP)
OFFERS THE FOLLOWING:

1. Information, referral, counseling, and community development activities for individuals, couples, families, groups, and communities in the city of Clairton and surrounding communities who have issues related to AOD use or misuse. Our approach in all areas of our work involves recognizing the family and social context of AOD use or misuse.
2. Our approach also recognizes the importance of collaboration and the strengthening of relationships and building social capital in addressing AOD

issues. Given that social capital involves the development of trusting, cooperative, mutual relationships, we seek to recognize power imbalances in all relationships. We address these imbalances whenever possible.

3. AA and NA meetings
4. Parenting counseling

THE CLAIRTON COMMUNITY OUTREACH PROGRAM (CCOP) STATEMENT OF PURPOSE:

The CCOP works with communities, families, and individuals to reduce isolation and build on strengths, to support people in making lifestyle and relationship choices and in managing conflict while reducing the harm associated with AOD usage.

The CCOP strongly believes that solutions or strategies for addressing conflict and drug issues are best addressed in an environment that enhances relationships. The development of trusting relationships at all levels of our community is vital to address drug and other related issues.

THE CLAIRTON COMMUNITY OUTREACH PROGRAM (CCOP) BELIEVES IN

1. the right of people to make choices in their own lives;
2. the right of people to dignity, respect, privacy, and confidentiality;
3. the right of people to be valued as individuals;
4. the right of people to access services on a nondiscriminatory basis; and
5. the right of the community to accountable and responsive services.

SERVICE DELIVERY:

1. To provide a specialized Alcohol and Other drug (AOD) counseling
2. To provide service to any and all people who come to our outreach program
3. To offer education and informal therapy through group work
4. To provide and disseminate an appropriate range of resource materials
5. To facilitate increased access to and/or use of support systems and

SERVICES:

1. To assess the needs of individuals and families in the local community
2. To foster education
3. To promote community awareness of AOD and family issues
4. To provide education and information on individual, family, and community issues related to AOD abuse

POLICY OR ADVOCACY:

1. To advocate for the provision of comprehensive, high-quality, family-focused AOD services
2. To advocate and influence public policy development in regard to the issues surrounding AOD usage with respect to the family and the wider community
3. To develop networks in Clairton, Pennsylvania, to assist families experiencing problems associated with AOD usage

RESOURCE MANAGEMENT:

1. To develop and maintain a flexible, innovative, dynamic organization which is efficient and effective and which values the people involved in it
2. To ensure appropriate support and professional development for our staff, volunteers, and management committee members so as to provide a professional service for anyone who enters our facility
3. To broaden the networks that supports the organization and its mission

OUR COUNSELING SERVICES:

We recognize alcohol and other drug use can be a problem in itself as well as a symptom of other issues. We, therefore, work with our clients to identify the many issues that that they believe relate to their AOD use or misuse. These could include domestic violence, child protection, housing, mental health, isolation, family conflict, peer pressure, employment, and poverty.

We provide informal counseling to the individual user, family member, or the whole family as needed. The issues clients present are very complex; we, therefore, work with a number of agencies to support our clients to address AOD, domestic violence, child protection, housing, mental health, and other issues. This work includes advocating for their needs to be met. We have an eclectic approach and use a range of modalities when working with clients. We provide groups for individual users and family members.

We aim to provide more collaborative services with other organizations and design and develop clinical services that may be center-based as well as at other locations in Clairton, Pennsylvania.

OUR COMMUNITY DEVELOPMENT ACTIVITIES:

We work collaboratively with many other organizations on projects. The CCOP also advocates influencing policy around family, relationships, and AOD issues.

CCOP hopes in coordinating strategies that aims to strengthen the ability and capacity of the city of Clairton to address relationship and AOD issues. The strategy seeks to address AOD issues through processes of empowerment that involve building a community and interagency team and supporting the skills development of community members and agency representatives. Participants engage in activities that promote a philosophy of cooperation and recognition of the context of drug use.

Groups and communities are facilitated to further engage in additional activities that address AOD issues within this philosophy. This project is an ambitious large-scale organic project.

CCOP promotes itself as a small community organization that develops and maintains cooperative relationships and addresses our own goals at the same time as common goals for the community and network of organizations. Our activities will also be demonstrating how small community organizations can facilitate innovative and large-scale activities through strengthening relationships and working collaboratively with communities, other small community organizations, large nongovernment organizations, government, and business.

We will maintain the dignity and the ethical considerations on an individual basis. We will ensure the privacy of all individuals who enter our facility and manage their care according to the desire and goals that are set per individual. We will not violate any ethical concerns of any client seeking recovery.

The outreach program offers various programs with the intent to guide our members on a path of recovery, to challenge themselves to activities that they were never exposed to before. We desire to create positive life-defining moments through these activities, which we ultimately lead to an attachment to the norms of our vast society. Our programs span any age-group, starting with preschool children and spanning through the rest of the developmental stages. The programs that we offer are pathways through the invisible barriers that still exist within our society, such as racism, prejudices, and biases. Also, through our programs we intend to bring about awareness to all of our society of these inequalities. The educational standards will be heightened within our program center as well help the community at large develop a cultural identity of their own. Our hopes are to incorporate this proven model throughout society and perhaps global at some point. We have a variety of programs, such as:

PROGRAM BREAKDOWN

The CCOP is a community-based innovative, progressive nongovernment organization that works with individuals, families, groups, communities, and organizations to address AOD issues in Clairton, Pennsylvania. Our philosophy at the center is to offer a multifaceted approach to behavioral and mental disorders, and alcohol and substance abuse abstinence is necessary to achieve health and wellness. We are in essence a community within the inner city, and with this, our clients need only enter the front door of our facility to begin their journey to health and wellness. We believe that exposing our youth to the many different alternatives that exist outside of the inner city will create defining moments that will aid in combating deviant behavior.

ALCOHOL AND SUBSTANCE ABUSE SERVICES: IMPROVISATIONAL DRAMA CLUB

This program offers the community adolescents, and in some cases adults as well, to gain insight into the perspective of the actors who participate. This program will afford many assessments, and with this, valuable insight into the minds of our youth will be provided. The logic is that the skits that are being presented. Drug and alcohol abuse, gangbanging, teen pregnancies, to name a few, will project the perspectives from individuals who may have experienced these difficulties. Currently, we have twelve adolescent members, one counselor, and two volunteers. We also plan on attending professional plays and attending functions as such.

GOSPEL CHOIR:

This program was implemented in most part because we are a Christian-based facility. We acknowledge God, and the vast majority of our outreach program recognizes this. We do not judge, and we welcome all, regardless of the religious beliefs. This program will afford the members the opportunity to expand on their cultural experiences by the field trips, such as Broadway musicals, and will help in developing richness in their life that will aid in their health and wellness. Currently, we have ten members, and this number is growing daily.

PREMILITARY ENTRANCE TRAINING:
(THIS INCLUDES COMBATIVE MMA/BOXING.)

This innovative program will bring structure and discipline into the lives of many who are suffering from deviant behavior. We will instill traits such as honor, integrity, faith, discipline, and honesty through a rigid program geared toward the success of each involved.

ART CLUB:

This program is another program that offers richness to one's life. We are currently working on a project that is being led by Mr. Qualters, a renowned Pittsburgh artist, in placing a mural on our outside wall of our facility. We currently have twelve members in our art club, and we are growing daily.

AMATEUR BOXING:

This program helps the individual to learn words such as honor, integrity, discipline, and respect. We implement a training regimen that is intense and will afford our athletes the opportunity to advance in the sport of boxing to a professional level. We are sanctioned through Colorado Springs and are one of the best boxing gyms in the country.

THE PREOPERATIONAL STAGE OF DEVELOPMENT PROGRAM:

This program was created in been in January of 2009. We have surveyed the population of the city of Clairton, and many are very excited with this new and exciting approach toward educating our children between the ages of three to six. The identity of self is the target goal of the CCOP, and with this we will develop within our members a sense of pride, value, and moral standards, along with a higher form of educational methods to ensure positive growth. The diverse cultural values and the willingness of change will help bring about these necessary values toward a healthy lifestyle void of deviant behavior. This program is geared toward establishing structure, learning respect for oneself and for others, and promoting a sound relationship between the mind and body connections.

INTERVENTIONS AT THE CCOP:
PERSONNEL WHO HAVE EXPERIENCED THIS LIFESTYLE

The individual who has experienced life within the inner cities will have greater success with guiding a resident toward and through the path to recovery. The success rate of the counselors who have experienced life within the inner city will be much greater than those of the counselors who have no experience within the inner city. This strategic intervention, using knowledgeable counselors, or experienced inner-city counselors, will prove to be quite effective. The logic behind this intervention is that the commonalities of both the counselor and the client will greatly enhance the counselor's insight into what the client's current mind-set is and what the motivation behind the client's deviance is. The client will also hold the experienced counselor who has experienced inner-city life with great regard. Using ex-cons will intensify the recovery process of the deviants immensely, although this statement may come across as being slightly irrational. The older ex-con, the individual who has paid the price for his or deviance, such as prison time, is considered a role model in the eyes of a deviant. These ex-cons are referred to as "old heads" in the streets.

The CCOP staff consists of four old heads, and with the proper guidance, these old heads have helped tremendously with the recovery of quite a few deviants. What is interesting is that the counselor, who is from the inner cities, who might not have served time incarcerated, will gather much respect; however, when an old head places his stamp of approval on the leading counselor, this elevates the status of the counselor significantly. When the level of trust and respect is proportionate, meaning, both the respect levels from counselor to client and client toward counselor, then and only then will the counselor be effective. If an imbalance exists between these two, the therapeutic attempt toward recovery will not happen. All is lost.

THE INITIAL ASSESSMENT IS VERY IMPORTANT.

We do not treat our facility as a mental health clinic; many would be offended by this. The offensive nature of stating that an individual may not be approaching life in a competent way could be interpreted by the deviant or resident as being less than normal, weak, or even disturbed. We as professionals know this is not the case. The inner-city dwellers, the majority of them, will not see it this way. We have to be mindful that pride is one thing that cannot be taken away from them, the residents. And to further this, many of the residents within the inner cities do realize that while they may not be book smart, their street savvy is considered their educational equivalent to a college-educated individual. This is the balance we as counselors have to be aware of, and to state that mental health counseling is needed to further positive growth will be met with much resistance.

Initially, and to compensate for this mind-set, we as counselors have to take a hard stance, almost argumentative, in our educational expertise. We have to make them understand that they are not mentally less than us, that we are only trying to open their eyes to new ways of viewing life that their intelligence should allow them to be open to new pathways that they have been denied because of the many inequalities that exist. We may have to go as far as enlightening them of the many great and successful individuals who were born and raised within the inner cities and how they achieved this greatness. In short, cultural education may be needed.

We must be able to speak our mind in terms they, the deviants and residents of the inner cities, understand—street jargon. Being completely honest as to what we are trying to do and why and that we expect complete honesty in return. At the CCOP, if we catch someone lying, they are banned from our facility for a week or two.

This posture and conduct of the counselor within the inner city must be established at the onset, the initial assessment. If the client does not respond well to this approach, the counselor may need to reassess their posture. If you are seen as weak or, as stated from the street perspective, soft, the client will not accept you as worthy. The need to reassert your posture may be needed. To do this, let the client speak in depth, listen attentively, always looking into the eyes, and be aware of your visual clues, as well as your active listening. The client will disclose eventually the weaknesses that he or she sees in you, and then readjustment will be possible.

ACKNOWLEDGE TO OUR MEMBERS THAT THERE ARE INEQUALITIES THAT EXIST.

The sooner we can express our beliefs that inequalities do exist and that racism, prejudices, and biases are barriers that need to be overcome, the more effective the sessions will be. We have to make are clients understand that we are here to knock down these barriers so as to expose our members to new and exciting cultural and educational experiences. This could be as simple as going to an art museum or as extreme as going skydiving.

This acknowledgment is extremely important, more so if the counselor is of another race than the client. This intervention will demonstrate respect and understanding, which will lead to a greater appreciation and respect toward the counselor.

PROVIDING DISCIPLINED AND MOTIVATIONAL RESOURCES

Our amateur boxing program is an area of great interest, and this is where the CCOP is most effective. This is so effective because of our trainers, which we have four of. One is a marine (Mr. Hodish), who has been involved in boxing for forty-five years, two are army rangers, and one was in the air force. We bring extreme discipline; we have a quote from the marines that is to be memorized by our athletes: "Discipline is the instant willing obedience to orders and self-respect." Also, every trainer has much experience in boxing; and when an individual is feeling mean, being that this is a contact sport, there are many people who will oblige another in a friendly and supervised sparring session.

This is the CCOP's way of instilling pride and discipline; this does not mean to suggest that this is the only means of instilling pride and discipline. The counseling approach should be unique; however, providing this is necessary, a resource of interest that will instill discipline for those who would be considered deviant.

MEMBERS OR CLIENTS ARE TO BE COURTEOUS AND APPRECIATIVE.

This intervention is used to enhance a positive relationship. We as counselors have to be mindful that respect should never be demanded but earned. However, initially do not be surprised to find yourself with the perception that you are being disrespected by the language or terminology or at times the forthright posture of your client. Keep in mind that in many cases, the use of vulgar language, or street jargon, is not used so much as a means of disrespect; on the contrary, there may be times when this language could be meant as a sign of appreciation. Make a serious effort to be knowledgeable of the terminologies of the community that you are in.

Establishing an understanding from the onset of a counseling session of the expected behavior of the client is highly recommended. Also, explaining these expectations that are required from the client. If you have a handout of these expectations, that would be the suggested approach, reading word for word the expectations to the client. Once these expectations are understood clearly and the client acknowledges that these expectations are completely understood, do not hesitate to point out if and when one of these expectations is violated. This intervention will help in the process of building a respectful relationship as well as establishing a sense of discipline.

DRUG AND ALCOHOL PREVENTION

If a client comes into the office and is perceived to be using drugs or is presenting the use of alcohol consumption, regardless of the amount of either the drugs or alcohol, this client needs to be asked to leave the establishment immediately.

At the onset of admittance of a client, the initial assessment, the precise course of action when a client comes into the establishment or counseling office while using either drugs or alcohol needs to be clearly stated with a handout for the client stating the same.

Do not hesitate to explain that the police will be contacted immediately and that counseling sessions will be terminated for a period of two weeks for this violation. Many will find this practice to be unethical; however, we always have to be mindful that we are working within the inner cities, specifically where the presence of gangs is, and this intervention can ultimately save lives. An example of how this can be played out is that allowing the client to enter once into your office and/or establishment and providing counseling will demonstrate to this client that you are weak or soft and will continue this practice. With this allowance, your limits will be tested by the using client, and if this client senses weakness, he or she will test your limits further. Do not let this happen as this can become dangerous. Asking the client to leave immediately will help prompt respect, and if the client returns for further counseling, rest assured, he or she will not return using.

We at the CCOP, if we find drugs on or near (we have claimed a two-block radius) our facility, we will confiscate these drugs, and a call to the police will come. This happens often, and while many would think that retaliation is forthcoming from the gang in Clairton, the residents in Clairton realize that we are only trying to help, that we are genuine and caring, so this retaliation never comes.

AVAILABILITY

This should depend on each counselor, as we all have our own life, and many of us will not be able to afford this undefined timeframe of availability. We at the CCOP are available 24/7 and will make an enormous effort to help in any way possible, including help in school work, job searches, job interviews. Any and all services needed, one need only ask. This elevates the level of respect tremendously, and with this, our success rate climbs accordingly so.

Anyone entering into this specific arena of MH Counseling and has a desire to work within the inner city should be very careful. This is not an area that is comfortable by any means. There is much heartache, and there are more negative experiences than there is positive. Having an association or a great familiarity with the residents within the inner city is advisable as there are many dangers when one is not known. Confronting known gangbangers is very dangerous, and without being known and accepted can lead to serious harm or possible death.

THE ALTERATION OF PERCEPTION THEORY: FORMATION OF THE INNER-CITY MENTALITY: JOHN HODISH (2006)

When discussing the alteration of perception theory (Hodish 2008), this theory points directly to our conscious and unconscious mind; and through our conscious and unconscious state of mind, our perceptions can be changed. The individual whose perception is in need of change must be accepting of this modification. This alteration will occur with education, lifestyle, and physical and mental adaptation. The goal of this change is to establish a perception of well-being.

The altering perceptions theory suggests that mental activity is a constant and that awareness will emerge upon the awakening of our senses. In order for information to be processed, our senses or at least the sense that corresponds to the information that is being processed would have to be aware. An example of this could be an individual who is trying to put to memory information or data that is of importance; he or she may listen to a recorded format of this information while trying to sleep by wearing headphones. If, however, subliminal processing would be to suggest that we process information while all of our senses are awakened, and an unobserved memory is processed, this should not be considered a form of unconsciousness processing. Rather this activity should be considered typical memory processing. Being unconscious would reflect a loss of awareness and, with this, a loss of retention. We are no longer aware. A loss of consciousness and memory retention may occur.

"How good is the mind at extracting meaning from stimuli of which one is not consciously aware?" (Greenwald, Klinger, and Schuh 1995) The unconscious mind is defined by Bargh and Morsella (2008), pertaining to the cognitive psychological viewpoint, as "subliminal information processing—extracting meaning from stimuli of which one is not consciously aware" (pp. 73-79). This is a very interesting concept in that this would suggest an unconscious awareness and an awareness of self.

Consciousness is the compilation of our experiences and our emotional state of mind pertaining to each experience throughout a lifetime. Consciousness in every human being is hidden. It is enshrouded by our emotions, and these emotions are distinctly involved with each and every individual experience that we have had.

Consciousness has also been defined as a state of awareness, our awakened state of mind. This definition is just the starting point of our consciousness and should not be used as an explanation as to what consciousness is. The global workspace theory created by Bernard Baars (1988) would suggest that consciousness is to be thought of as "a limited resource capacity or module that enables information to be 'broadcast widely throughout the system and allows for more flexible sophisticated processing'" (p. 2).

This is very similar to the alteration of perceptions theory in that the term "broadcast" would reflect inner perception, which is used in the alteration of perception theory. However, the difference of these two theories is that according to the theory of alterations of perceptions, which suggests that consciousness does not stop at being a broadcast module, consciousness is in fact the essence of who we are. The appreciation of the global broadcast theory however does exist; seemingly this theory relies on "flexible sophisticated processing" (Baars 1988, 2) which this statement is undefined.

Consciousness is an emergence of self and continues to grow throughout a life span; this would be continued growth of our perceptions and the physical and emotional changes throughout our lives (Hodish 2006). However, the essence of our perceptions will stay the same, which will be either positive or negative, pointing directly to our social morality codes and our lawful societal ethics.

Sigmund Freud stated that "the conscious mind is what you are aware of at any particular moment, your present perceptions, memories, thoughts, fantasies, feelings, what have you" (Straker 2002, 2010). This statement of Freud is also very similar to the theory of alteration of perceptions theory except for the usage of the word "awareness."

Before we continue with the discussion of consciousness and unconsciousness, an understanding of awareness has to be broached. Awareness when discussing the theory of alterations of perceptions would be defined as the awakening of our consciousness.

Awareness is the focus for our conscious thoughts, and awareness, basing this on an individual perception, would make this individual's focus relative to his or her needs, desires, likes, or dislikes. A simple way to think of awareness would be to use an example: Families living in a financially depressed society who have never experienced life outside of their confines are not aware of how to dress for a night at the opera because they have never experienced this type of event. The financially depressed are not aware of mannerism of upper-class society because they have never experienced life in this manner. While they may be familiar with these things, their awareness of certain areas is stunted because they have not experienced this type of living. Their focus, or sense of awareness, is on the ideas, values, morals, wants, and desires that they can relate to. To expand on awareness a bit further, being aware of the wildlife in Africa is a fleeting thought for people who have never been there. This slight display of knowledge. Wildlife in Africa does not constitute awareness. This just demonstrates a learned reality. the emergence of self upon consciousness brings about awareness.

Our inner perspective is manifested through consciousness. This manifestation occurs at an age during the toddler stage, when the formation of memories and imagination begins to develop. This is how we acquire our own unique personality. Piaget who identified the four stages of cognitive development stated that during the "pre-operational stage (toddler and early childhood) intelligence is demonstrated through the use of symbols, language use matures, and memory and imagination are developed, but thinking is done in a non-logical, nonreversible manner; egocentric thinking predominates" (Huitt and Hummel 2003).

Our inner perspective cannot and will not ever be shared. This would be impossible because of the entanglement of emotions based on our own experiences from the day we were born up until the present has created this intangible. The inner perception can be thought of as our unspeakable thoughts.

Our outer perspective, which people can identify with, is seen uniquely through our eyes, and this perspective can be shared. The outer perspective is the ensemble of our inner perspective and the expectations of societal views and moral ethics. This outer perspective defines who we are in the eyes of others. Are we angry, are we thoughtful, are we happy, and are we approachable? These types of characteristics are displayed in our personalities.

When we consider why people do the things that they do, we try to scrutinize specific areas of their life: What was their childhood like? Were they loved? Is there a chemical imbalance within them? Were they aggressive their whole life? These would be questions that one may be asked if they were discussing a criminal mind. If we were to discuss a scholar, we may ask the following: Were his or her parents stern in their educational values? Was he or she from a strict upbringing? Was he or she loved? Did he or she have guidance?

The compilation of experiences of a person can never be dissected to obtain the answers to the questions that were stated, not immediately anyway, and may take years and years of study to understand the perception of just one individual.

EXAMPLE 1

For instance, some newborns will lie in a crib that provides warmth, tenderness. And a sense of comfort is present—a musical mobile spinning gently with Disney characters swirling back and forth—stimulating the sense of sight with smiles on the faces of these Disney characters. The newborn's room is painted in a soft blue or pink pastel color, and the odor of this living quarter is sweet, a fragrance of roses perhaps, permeating the sense of smell. Feeling the soft blanket that wraps them in warmth, the sense of touch is stimulated by the softness of the fabric. A mother is telling her husband good bye and kissing him gently on the cheek and saying I love you. These stimulate the sense of hearing. These are the ideal living conditions.

EXAMPLE 2

If we were to view this scenario in a different environment, such as the ghetto or the projects within the inner city, the mental processes and/or the retention of these different memories will have a profound effect on the newborn's behavior.

Bringing a newborn child home after birth into an environment such as a ghetto could be different:

The child may not have a crib or playpen, and the child may have to sleep on a couch or the bed with the parents or, in some cases, on the floor. The bed is old and very used. The cleanliness of this environment is terrible. The floors are very dirty. The walls have not been painted in years. And stains of all sorts are throughout the whole three-room apartment. There is no musical mobile of Disney characters hanging above the crib, the bedding is not soft, and the smell is not sweet. Cigarette smoke permeates the apartment, as does the smell of marijuana and alcohol and, in many cases, crack cocaine. The mother does not have a husband and is raising this child on her own. And while this example may sound exaggerated, there are many like this, some even worse, and some slightly better.

Unconsciously, the senses of a child are being stimulated, subliminally, and retention of memory is forming at the unconscious level; however, when awareness is present and the child is in the learning process, the foundation of many positive or negative attributes have already been laid. This is to suggest that retaining memories at the unconscious level is the foundation of our innermost perspectives, the building blocks of self. However, a certain amount of awareness does exist and transits through the unconscious stage. With that being said, awareness begins at the outer portion of our unconsciousness, the pinnacle between consciousness and awareness. This is where self will begin. (Refer to the illustration.)

As a child traverses through their environment, many outside factors can and will influence many behavioral characteristics. The positive influential growth can be sustained by providing a steady input of positive knowledge into this child's growth.

Using this example, example two, we will provide the necessary input for using the alteration of perception theory. We will try to understand that many of the inner-city dwellers only know one way of living. Imagine if you will that as a newborn you were born into an environment such as that described in example two. Your senses are being calloused from the time you took your first breath in your new environment.

"Calloused" would be defined as your senses accepting this negative input, and simply put, getting used to all of the negativity around you and accepting this as the truth of how life really is. Because many inner-city dwellers never leave their confines and explore nor are they exposed to the richness of life outside of these self-imposed boundaries, their callousness is thickened over time.

Territorial Instinct: The Balance of Equality: True Integration

An interesting phenomenon that had occurred was the formation of gangs, and what is shocking is that the territorial instinct that these gangs hold are, in part, a reason the expansion of personal growth is being limited. For instance, while the inner-city gangs who live deep inside of the confines of this brick-and-mortar prison are trying to get out, they cannot because of fear of being caught by rival gangs and being physically assaulted and maybe murdered. And the gangs who reside on the fringes of the inner city are maintaining their borders and at times are trying to get the inside of the inner city for expansion so their growth is also being stunted. The people who have no gang affiliations and are living within the inner city have a tremendous and horrifying experience because they are being harassed as to why they have no gang affiliation or they are being assaulted because they do not have a gang affiliation—the trap.

We as a society have to realize that until we have a balance of equality. Nothing will ever change as far as inner-city deviant behavior is concerned. The integration of these inner-city dwellers into an environment that is accepted by most in our society as a community of sound moral and ethical foundations needs to occur; however if this integration should ever occur, the population of inner-city dwellers would have to be dispersed in such a way that gang affiliations would no longer exist. Knowing that this integration is highly unlikely for all of the obvious reasons. Another approach is possible—altering perceptions.

The hoods and ghettos have to be torn down, and the inner-city population would have to have a new place of residency—urban redevelopment. However, this urban redevelopment would have to be single-abode family housing spread throughout the surrounding communities. The true meaning of integration has to occur, and the government would have to cover the cost, our way of expressing concern and also an extension of our understanding of the brutality imposed on African-Americans throughout their history within the United States. If we as a society could acknowledge and offer true integration, we as a society would reap the benefits of a true America. The benefits would be peace of mind, love of our brothers and sisters of all races, and harmony throughout our country, for the most part.

The majority of residents that reside in row houses, projects, ghettos, or slums, offer the same standard of living—block after block of abnormal behavior. These streets, blocks, and hoods will undoubtedly have some form of amalgamation within each area of concern from the perspectives of each deviant group; and while the shared interest that spans across these neighborhoods are the same, financial security and a certain level of social status, albeit deviant, this standard is obtained through gang warfare protecting their own area of the hood. This behavior presents the problem of expansion, which is needed for personal growth. Many are imprisoned within these protected boundaries.

These streets are not the standards of America or, should be said, not the moral and ethical way that the ideology of our forefathers, white America, perceived this to be. The guarded street, which ironically is stunting the personal growth of many of our citizens within our country, is another method in which the monster that we created is being nurtured.

What we have encountered now is a phenomenon that is killing many of our young society. Black-on-black crime is the end result until expansion of these gangs or terrorists finally reach out past these self-imposed boundaries and bite the hand that created them.

Also, the inequalities that extend outside of these ghettos, hoods, and slums are a welcoming committee that offers prejudice, hate, and racism. This is not to say that all of America is divided into inner city and suburbs; however the expansion of these hoods is not going to be acceptable, and violence will reach past the self-imposed borders of these hoods. We as a society have to welcome the inner-city dwellers with love, compassion, and understanding. We Americans have to tame this beast; we have to acknowledge the horrendous acts that were imposed on this subculture, and we have to rebuild our trusts.

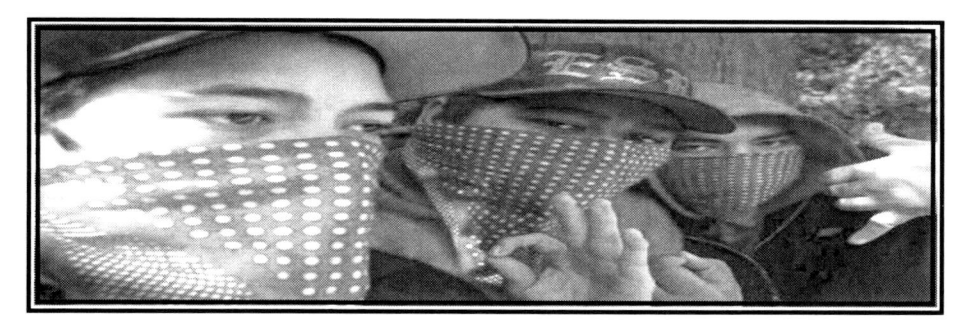

We as a society that pride ourselves on a nation of peace, reaching out to our global communities and imposing our way of life into their communities have to recognize the fact that we are losing lives in our own country by terrorists. American-made terrorists, the Bloods, Crips, and countless others are running amuck with no regard for the safety of others. If this terroristic display was happening in another country, we would certainly send a force to this country in order to maintain peace . . . but not on our own soil.

Some people may find the use of the term "terrorism" in describing the phenomenon of gang members and their acts. However, seeing a group of individuals running through the streets of any city with a variety of firearms, killing not only what they would consider their ememies but innocent bystanders, all the while concealing their identity with handkerchiefs or some sort of apparatus to hide themselves, is in fact terrorizing our society. Alan Krueger, in his book *What Makes a Terrorist: Economics and the Roots of Terrorism,* suggests that "poverty and lack of education have been the conventional scapegoats. And while they may have some impact, there is little empirical evidence supporting this claim. Instead, his analysis shows that political oppression and a lack of civil liberties are the principal culprits." The reason that there is little empirical evidence is the lack of effort concerning this topic within in our own borders of the United States, and while this may hold true with political terrorist, this is not the case within the United States. An argument does exist within Alan Krueger's book in most part due to his one-sided definition of what terrorism truly is. Terrorism does not have to be political, and if we would to broaden the scope of terrorism, we would find that what Krueger is suggesting is the truth. However, all of the components have to be considered equally. Poverty and education holds an equal part in the nurturing of terrorism within our own country of the United States.

The nature of this beast, the formation of many gangs, is due to commonalities that exist between people who are experiencing life in an area that offers less than the norms of the greater populace, and with the economy struggling in the twentieth century, the expansion of these gangs are going to grow. Now is the time to divide these groups and spread them throughout the country, offering them the benefits that are due to them—an honest living and the respect they deserve.

Inequalities do not exist, pertaining to inner-city dwellers, because the greater society does not perceive these inequalities to exist or the greater society finds this phenomenon easier to forget. We as a society afforded these people the existence of just being, initially, and offered inner-city dwellers nothing except freedom to be ignored, hated because of race, and prejudice, racism and bias. The inequalities that exist within the inner city occur in various forms such as education, health and political participation, as well as income.

Educational balance would be a good start. We as a society would also have to be very strict and disciplined also if we were to distribute the government funding of our schools equally across this country. The educational systems would also have to have the right to implement a stronger disciplinary recourse for those students who do not comply with the new standards of education, as well as the parent or parents of this child.

To address these dimensions of poverty, we need solidarity in which all persons are accountable for a common good that advances the equal dignity and freedom of all citizens. Trying to find scholarly articles as to support the claims that inner-city schools are suffering from many inequalities is like finding a needle in a hay stack. This alone should be indicative as to the interest of the educational community pertaining to the necessity of an equal educational standard; however, and in fact, this lack of research is support enough. While there are articles, journals, and books readily available to support certain and specific claims, they do not synthesize all claims; they are in actuality pinpointing certain areas of failure. This is not good enough. We as a society have to realize that the many variables that are supporting failure within the inner-city educational systems, which these specific topics of discussions are available, support a certain area that needs attention, minimizing the vastness of this problem.

The answer is not specific. The many variables that are associated with the inequalities within the inner-city schools are much deeply rooted than, let's say, outdated school books. Attempting to appease the inner-city residents by providing a free lunch program, whereas the food is only good enough if one were an inmate at the local prison, will not work. The inner-city residents, the caretakers, realize that the only way out of the confines of this brick-and-mortar prison is through education.

An interesting statistic had just developed within the school district of Clairton. I was extended an invitation to attend a meeting being held by a group of doctors. This group can be identified as Positive Deviance, an organization that is also trying to alleviate deviant behavior. However, they are concentrating mostly within the school environment. I was asked to attend this meeting with a panel of school directors, teachers, and various business owners (ma-and-pa shops) throughout the community. This group was looking for facilitators for their model of urban recovery. I agreed reluctantly. As stated earlier in this manuscript, this group of doctors', and to be specific, medical doctors', premise toward alleviating deviant behavior was that one should use the resources that are available within the confines of the inner city in which they live, that the facilitators should be available to spread the word of right and wrong and to guide these deviants toward a path of righteousness. The concept is brilliant. However, the faulty assumption being made is that in essence, we are extending a message. This message being to settle for a state of mediocrity and to be complacent with their lives. This goes against all that I believe in. The inner-city adolescents, and even the older population, should always reach for the stars.

The interesting statistic that came about just recently was that the city of Clairton had its highest graduation rate thus far, graduating ninety-eight of their senior class. As I read this statistic, my stomach churned. I became very distraught and was sickened, literally. One would wonder why such a wonderful statistic could have such a negative effect.

At the meeting that was held, just two paragraphs above, a white teacher stated that she had a student, a black student, who had just weeks to go before graduation. This student had been skipping classes and when present was disruptive and was surely to fail. However, and as stated by this teacher, she thought outside of the box and approached this student and stated that if he would attend her class for the rest of the year without being disruptive, never missing a class in the weeks remaining, she would pass him; and she did.

I was appalled by this! Just simply amazed that an educator would do such a thing! I told this educator that I was in complete disagreement with how she handled this student. The other teachers and school administrators quickly jumped to her defense; and the doctors of the group Positive Deviance, because of their higher education, tried in vain to undermine this whole ordeal. I left, and I never returned.

Poverty is of the greatest concern; and while this manuscript focuses on the African-Americans, as explained earlier, this group was used because of the inner city in which I live. Inner cities that are poverty-stricken suffer the same fate throughout our society, whether it be white, Asian, or black. As stated by Servaas van der Berg (2008), "Poverty is not simply the absence of financial resources. According to Amartya Sen, poverty is the lack of capability to function effectively in society. Inadequate education can thus be considered a form of poverty" (p. 5). And to extend this further, the form of poverty that exists within the inner city of Clairton and in many inner cities throughout our society can be viewed as absolute poverty, again, as stated by Servaas van der Berg (2008):

> [A]bsolute poverty—the absence of adequate resources—hampers learning through poor nutrition, health, home circumstances (lack of books, lighting or places to do homework) and parental education. It discourages enrolment and survival to higher grades, and also reduces learning in schools (p. 5).

As I was walking out of the school, in a huff I might add, I noticed within the corridors, in the library, and even in the classrooms the absence of African-American leaders and role models throughout the history of the Unites States were missing from the hangings on the walls, and while the student body of this educational facility is predominantly black, all that was visible, the vast majority of hangings, were of the white culture.

Education is the key in raising the inner city up to a standard of living that would be acceptable by all. And while the strife of the continued struggle of complete equality will always be present, this would be the starting point. As stated by Servaas van der Berg (2008), "Education can reduce poverty in a number of ways, more educated people are more likely to get jobs, are more productive, and earn more" (p. 5).

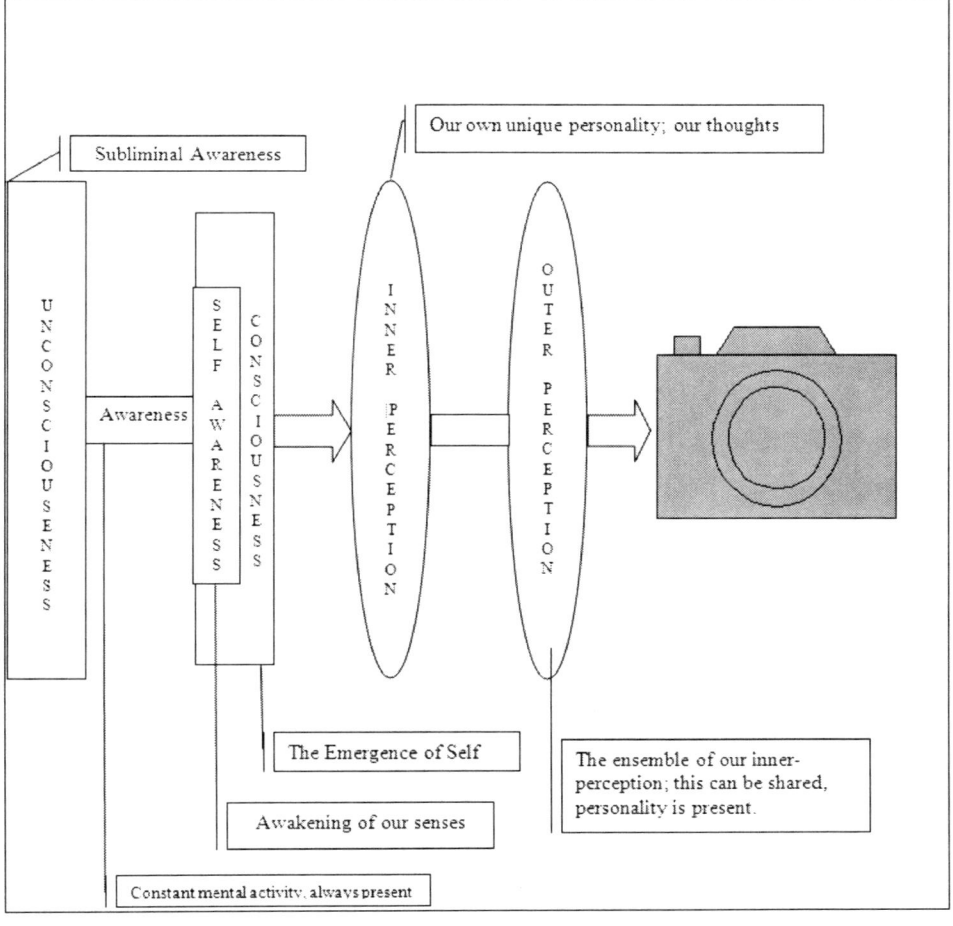

Subliminal Awareness

Our own unique personality; our thoughts

UNCONSCIOUSENESS

Awareness

SELF AWARENESS

CONSCIOUSNESS

INNER PERCEPTION

OUTER PERCEPTION

The Emergence of Self

Awakening of our senses

The ensemble of our inner-perception; this can be shared, personality is present.

Constant mental activity, always present

ALTERING PERCEPTIONS THEORY BY JOHN HODISH

Placing ourselves into an environment at any age will eventually alter our attitudes in many areas of self-awareness; however, being born into an environment, and enduring all of the negative and positive aspects of said environment, will in fact cement our resolve toward a culture that is conducive for survival.

Reverting back to what this study is in reference to, inner-city dwellers and deviant behavior, the perceptions of many inner-city dwellers is based on self-awareness and the methods of survival in this environment. The hostilities of this environment stem from years of neglect, from outside sources that spawned ignorance and hatred from years gone by.

In order to change the perspectives of inner-city dwellers, we would have to alter this lifestyle; and to do this, mass integration would have to occur. Presenting a truly integrated society is the most important part of altering perception. While this alteration of perceptions would span generations, ultimately, and throughout the course of this concept, the likelihood of reducing crime would be reduced; although crime may spread into the suburbs initially, this phenomenon would soon fade when characteristics such as ethics and moral justification occurs. Although integration is not meant to reflect white supremacy in any manner, these characteristic traits, such as morality and ethics (this is not to suggest that African-Americans are less moral or have no ethical traits; this is to ensure proper integration of all aspects pertaining to the alterations of perceptions) can and should be incorporated into predominantly African-American communities. However, the social bonds of race would come much faster with a full integration, whether this means white America needs to make the transition or black Americans need to make the transition. Either way, the idea behind the alteration of perception theory is to justify the attitudes held by many African-Americans that white America was, and in some instances still is, trying to hold them down and that white America finally recognizes this dilemma and is going to adjust this wrong doing by affording a very large expense in order to balance the scales, not only financially but with moral fabric and ethical rights as well. This balance is long past due.

Integration is necessary for this nation to begin its ethical and moral climb back to where it once was, and until this need is approached, black-on-black crime will continue to rise. And in time, this crime will encapsulate our entire society, as it is already starting to happen. Inner-city dwellers have very little, and what this subculture does have will be defended with life and limb. The ghettos and slums have to be torn down. Urban redevelopment has to be a high priority, and these individuals have to be a priority as well. Employment, equivalent to ensure a standard of living that is equal to any other middle-class families, has to be the minimum financial award; and an education has to be given equal to any other educational system throughout our country. Equality has to be in its truest form. African-Americans also have an obligation as well while these rights should be given an expectation has to be met. African-Americans have to accept these changes, relocation into many white neighborhoods have to take place, and the protection that will definitely have to be in place have to be present. Many white Americans, along with many African-Americans, will rise against this radical approach; however, weathering this initial storm will be justified over the years.

The perception held by many inner-city dwellers has been so ingrained that this subculture has developed their own code of justice, their own morality code, and a perverted sense of ethics while we, the society that values a set of norms that is conducive to fellowship, care, and compassion, are bewildered by how this phenomenon can actually be occurring.

After interviewing hundreds of adolescent males, Caucasians and African-Americans who live in the inner city, the question was posed, "What is the goal of gangs or individuals who seek success without education or a job?" The common answers were money, power, and respect. This perspective is one that is fully ingrained in these young males. And all inner-city adolescent males and most adolescent females accept this as valid answers. The method as to how they achieve financial success is obvious, and I was often laughed at when I asked of these methods because they feel everyone knows the answer, and while I assumed this financial success was through deviant ways, I needed validity. The drug trade, prostitution, theft, and murder are all common ways for these inner-city dwellers to survive financially. Power comes from who has the most "juice" (this term is in reference to guns, the strongest gang, or the best connections pertaining to drugs) and whoever can survive; this usually refers to who does not die or who does not go to prison. He or she is usually the one who gains the most respect although many drug dealings happen behind prison walls and usually there are members from the same click behind prison walls so this phenomenon continues even after incarceration. As inner-city dwellers see this predicament, there is no way out, and the only means of gathering income to support their "own" is through urban warfare.

INEQUALITIES

DESPAIR AND HATE

DRUG AND ALCOHOL ABUSE

As can be seen by this illustration, and along with poverty, the inner-city dwellers feel hopeless and lost; they are confined to this brick-and-mortar prison, with very little hope of well-being. The avenues available to break free from this environment are slim. Unless we as a society realize what we have created and begin to correct our mistakes, our future will be filled with terror, and our standard of living will be affected greatly.

THE FORMATION OF DEVIANCE: CASE STUDY: JOHN HODISH: LIFE SPAN DEVELOPMENT

A single case study will be used to demonstrate how perceptions can be altered. However, a sense of awareness has to be present from the individual who is seeking change, and the need for this change must be a priority from the individual who is seeking change.

This case study will demonstrate how Erikson's stages of development (1902-1994) and Kohlberg's stages of moral development intertwined throughout this personal portrait of the author, John Hodish. Mr. Hodish's life will be analyzed, starting with his childhood and ending with his present state of self. We will see how his moral standards were developed and how his views on gender differences were formed. We will also convey how these factors can be elucidated within the framework of gender differences and environmental, cultural, and ethnic influences. This case study is an overall reflection of most inner-city dwellers, and while some individual cases may not be this severe, some are worse.

LIFE SPAN DEVELOPMENT PROJECT CHILDHOOD

For this project, I will be using myself. I was born on July 15, 1960, in the city of Clairton, Pennsylvania. I was the youngest of five children. The three oldest (listed chronologically) by age are my half sister Charlene Di'Liberatore; my half brother, Charles Di'Liberatore; and another half sister, Barbara Di'Liberatore. I had one full sibling; her name was Marie Hodish. The half-blood siblings were very young when their father died from a stroke, which affected my oldest half sister immensely. Charlene developed a hole in her heart after her father died, and her demeanor changed completely. She became very aggressive and lived a provocative lifestyle; this is according to what my mother claimed. Charlene, at the age of eighteen, became a stripper; and one night after work, she was raped by three men who were never tried for this offense. Charlene's attitude toward life became even worse, and she became violent toward my mother, and this was when the sexual abuse toward me began. I was five years old at the time this abuse first started. To complicate Charlene's dilemma, my mother sent her to a hospital for a mental evaluation; and although I do not know what her diagnosis was, I do know that she began receiving shock treatments, which left Charlene to a point where she was almost functionless.

I was born in McKeesport Hospital and was relatively healthy. My birth weight was seven pounds six ounces, and I was twenty-one inches long. The environment in which I was raised was terrible; my family was very poor and had a very hard time providing food, let alone clothing. The house was not heated for the first seven years of my life, and the living room in which I slept—on a couch (which pulled out to a bed)—had an iceberg in the corner of the room during winter. This big piece of ice stretched from ceiling to floor, with a width of four feet, and the base was roughly two and a half feet thick. Our diet consisted of apple butter, mustard, and ketchup sandwiches; French fries (because potatoes were inexpensive); and chicken made in a variety of ways. However, the chicken was not that often served. We never had vegetables, fruit, candy, or any kind of potato chips or pop; these items were nonexistent. We never ate at specific times. The only regular meals we had was if we were lucky enough to have a school meal, and the only way I could get a school meal is if I would beg other students for money.

When I was five years old (this is the earliest I can remember) up until I was thirteen years old, I suffered from every kind of abuse imaginable. This sexual abuse was inflicted on me by my oldest half sister; and the mental, physical, and verbal abuse came from my father for the most part. I had a very isolated childhood, referring to any type of positive interaction from my parents or siblings. Every situation that may have occurred during my young years as a child had to be resolved by me alone; I had no guidance in any aspect of my life other than the sport of boxing. My father was the one who introduced me to the sport of boxing, and this is the only contribution that he had made when considering my life. My zone of proximal development, which can be defined as "the difference between the level of performance when a child tries to accomplish a task independently as opposed to when the child receives guidance or instructions from an adult or peer" (Wertsch and Tulviste 1992), was never reached because of neglect of my parents. However, I do remember having a certain level of pride when it came to achievement of any type. According to Lev Vygotsky (1992), "Human development is an apprenticeship in which children advance when they collaborate with others who are more skilled." Vygotsky also claimed that "not much headway was achieved in development if the child walks this path alone." This assumption may be true in some cases, but this is not always the truth in other cases, specifically my case. I was aware of the wrongdoings that I was experiencing, and I can honestly say that my calculated escape from this terror was a plan that was devised at a very early age. I would have to agree with Piaget (1954) in that "children engage in a continual interaction with their environment" (p. 49). This was my method of development. I did however "develop the ability to try new things, and I also learned to accept failure with ease. This is the Initiative Versus Guilt psychosocial stage of development, from age three to six"

(Erikson and Erikson 1997, 40). However, I did not reach the "Industry versus Inferiority, six to adolescent stage of development" (Erikson and Erikson 1997, 40) until I was to the end of my adolescence. The industry versus inferiority stage is when we establish a sense of mastery and competence.

I received my first broken nose at the hands of my father at the age of five. I also endured cracked ribs, broken fingers, and almost death because of my parents' negligence. When I was just a baby, the door to the back porch was opened. I crawled out onto this porch, which had no siding; and I fell off, which was about a five-foot drop. I landed on my back, and I laid in this rainstorm for hours, finally discovered by my oldest half-brother. Because of this incident, I acquired double pneumonia: I could not hold any food down so I was fed intravenously. A priest was called in to give me my last rites. They tried for the last time to feed me, a needle in my head; and fortunately, this last attempt worked. My brother recounted this story and said I was less than two years old.

The community where I had grown up in was mostly African-American, and this time was the beginning of the civil rights movement. This was a very hard time for me, being that I am Caucasian. The aggression that was part of me because of my personal life was not conducive to passivity. I was in fistfights on a daily basis. The city of Clairton was in turmoil. This city was a war zone, and I was one of the main combatants. This is not to say that I was a racist, nor was I prejudiced; I was just angry. I grew up in a community of poverty, and my best friends were African-American; and this is the truth to this day. We in Clairton, it being a financially depressed community, have seen it all—drug and alcohol abuse, prostitution, murder, every crime imaginable. The school district, which at one time was at the top of the list academically, is now at the bottom of the list in Pennsylvania.

LIFE SPAN DEVELOPMENT PROJECT: MIDDLE CHILDHOOD

During my middle childhood years, "the formal-operational period, abstract reasoning, along with my hypothetical reasoning" (Bond 1995) was basically my salvation from a childhood filled with terror and pain. Being able to understand the reality of my problem at this young age and then being able to evaluate different scenarios on how to escape the torment that I was living through helped tremendously in my positive growth. An example of this formal-operational period would be a scenario that I thought of often during this time. I would often think of how I would become a terrific pugilist and how I would dedicate my life to this sport; I would become rich and famous, and with this fame and fortune, I would escape from this torment. This plan worked; I became intent on beating my father in our nightly sparring session, and after many bloody noses and a broken nose, I landed the big punch. The right cross that I landed hit my father squarely in his nose. I saw blood trickle out of his nose, and although I took a very serious beating and another broken nose, this was the last sparring session that we had. I often hoped that the reason my father stopped with the sparring was because of the punch that I landed, but this was not the reason. The reason was the severity of the beating that he gave me. I have remained active in the sport of boxing for forty-five years now, and I am currently in the process of making a decision on whether I want to accept a job offer from Colorado Springs to become their head coach for the U.S. boxing team. My plan worked.

My social relationships were nonexistent during my middle childhood years because of my aggressive behavior. My aggression was due to a very low self-esteem. The aggressive behavior that I was demonstrating lends itself to the social learning theory. With social learning theory, "people acquire aggressive responses the same way they acquire other complex forms of social behavior—either by direct experience or by observing others" (Bandura 1983, 2001; Mischel 1973, 1999; Mischel and Shoda 1995).

Children at this time of my development had a sense that I was different, that I was very poor, and that I was troubled. I did not fit into the norm that most children this age were experiencing. My family life was filled with abuse, which took a tremendous toll on my relationships with my siblings. We all had our own escapes. The two oldest siblings, Charlene and Chucky, were never home, in most part because of the obvious abuse that was happening on a daily basis. They tended to ignore it. The middle child, Barbara, began experimenting with drugs at this time, stayed in her attic loft to keep away from the abuse she was experiencing from our mother. And the youngest daughter who was two years older than me, was experiencing verbal, mental, and physical abuse from our mother so she had her own dilemma.

There was very little interaction among the siblings, and when there was any type of interaction, it was in the context of arguing for the most part. There was on occasion an attempt made by my parents to try and interact with me and my youngest sister, Marie, by playing a board game or cards, but these times failed miserably, often ending in an argument or an attack by my father on me. An example of this was when I and my sister were teammates in Monopoly against my father and mother, and we were winning. My father landed on Boardwalk, which put them in a very bad position; they were bordering on losing the game at this point. I started to chuckle so he picked up the game board and smacked it against the side of my head then made me pick up all of the pieces of the game and put the game away. At this point, I felt hatred like never before.

After the incident of the Monopoly game, my aggressive behavior worsened, and I began to get in fistfights at school on a daily basis. My math teacher, Mrs. Albert, took a special interest in me; and while she knew of my abuse, she never questioned me. She introduced me to the school guidance counselor; and between these two people, we began my road to recovery. They showed me the beauty in people, the love and compassion that some people do have. This was the turning point in my life. They taught me understanding, patience, and gentleness. Although this transformation took quite some time, two years perhaps, it was the beginning. Mrs. Albert, whom the other children thought was terribly mean, along with the guidance counselor, made an enormous impact in my life.

Mrs. Albert helped in ushering me into what I believe would be my "Intimacy versus Isolation stage of development." This stage of development prepared me to, as stated by Erikson and Erikson (1997), "reach out and connect with others" (p. 40). This time of my life was the turning point in which I could have gone one of two ways—a life of crime or who I am today, a compassionate and law-abiding citizen.

LIFE SPAN DEVELOPMENT PROJECT: ADULTHOOD

Entering adulthood was not an easy transition; I still harbored an aggressive behavior. Using the five-factor model developed by Paul Costa Jr. and Robert McCrae (in press, as cited in reference), my adulthood began high in the neuroticism dimension. "Being anxious was due in most part of my lack of ability to reach out to others or not knowing how to. The desire to have normal friendships was necessary to me; acceptance was crucial. My hostilities stemmed not only from not being accepted but off my self-consciousness of my family environment and the abuse that I received from family members. I became depressed, impulsive, and vulnerable" (Costa and McCRae, in press, as cited in reference).

The normalcy that I was looking for did not happen until I was in my mid-twenties. This transition occurred when I joined the U.S. Marine Corps. This was when I entered my "extraversion dimension." Being that most of the recruits at Paris Island, the Marine Corps Training Depot came from similar backgrounds, I was finally accepted among my peers; and I excelled. Being promoted upon completion of basic training is something every recruit strives for and only three receive. During the extraversion stage of development, I came out of my shell because of the environment in which I was in. I was among, and part of, the world's greatest fighting force: I was home. "I had boundless energy. I was thrust into a leadership role where stressing my opinion was not only desired but necessary" (Costa and McCRae, in press, as cited in reference). The marines offered a challenging environment in which I excelled.

Upon my discharge from active duty, I took with me many positive attributes; however, I also gained many negative ones also. I was taught in the marines how to channel my fears into a destructive force, to conquer my enemy, and with this knowledge and my personal history, I almost became disastrous. Not only could I fight, I had no moral obligation to society, or so I felt.

I was on the way toward a lifestyle enriched with joy and happiness, but I was not quite there yet. I did not get into trouble as much as I did before upon my tour in the marines, but I was still looking to "test my metal" (a marine Corps ideology of applying what we learned during combat). However, I had no enemy.

Fortunately, I found the love of my life, my wife, during this time; and my desire to test my metal was not that important anymore, thank goodness. My desire to impress my wife during our courtship outweighed my desire to test my metal, and this led me into my "openness to experience dimension" (Costa and McCRae, in press, as cited in reference). I used to take my wife to work almost every day, and being laid-off from my job at this time afforded me the opportunity of personal growth. I would go to the museums during the day while my wife worked, and I developed a strong sense of appreciation for the arts. My thoughts of the wonderful life that my future wife and I were embarking on carried me into a sense of calm that I have never experienced before. I often asked my wife why she chose me, and she always said "You are a wonderful man, the best man I have ever known," which strengthened my resolve to be the best man I possibly could for this magnificent woman.

From the time that I had met my wife up until the present, a desire to help others, specifically children and adolescents, became an obsession; I have entered the "agreeableness dimension, which is simply defined as being cooperative and polite" (Costa and McCRae, in press, as cited in reference). I have always had a boxing gym, and the priority of this gym was not so much the sport of boxing but to offer myself and my experiences to the young in the hopes of steering them from the mistakes that I have made. To give them hope and solutions to any problem that they may have was my goal.

Recently, the city of Clairton, where I was born and raised, extended itself to further my commitment to the young and old alike of our community; they offered me a building, and they pay for the utilities. This community outreach program, while amateur boxing is the focus, is geared more toward aiding others in their time of need. We offer individual counseling, family counseling, employment placement, educational assistance, and personal and spiritual growth; I have never been so happy.

I was employed at Auberly's, a placement shelter for troubled teens; I was a counselor for twenty adolescents. This place of employment increased my level of consciousness to a high in which I never could have imagined. This level has motivated me to the point where I cannot receive enough education; my level of education will never be enough.

Throughout my life, I have sacrificed, lived in blackness, negativity at every turn, and somehow, with the grace of God and an instinct for survival, I succeeded; I am truly blessed. From Mrs. Albert, the guidance counselor, into the marines, and my beautiful wife, this was my salvation.

Coming from an abusive childhood, being poor, and enduring a tumultuous life span, specifically early childhood and throughout my adolescence, I had views on life that were quite distorted. My emotional state of mind was absent, and I had no interest in the concerns of others. As I grew into my early adulthood, I became extremely focused: stage five of Erikson's stages of development, ego identity versus role confusion; I knew exactly what I needed in my life and how I was going to grow into a respectable and productive being in society. I developed a sense of self (Erikson 1990).

VIEWING MY PERSONAL GROWTH, ACCORDING TO ERIKSON'S STAGES OF DEVELOPMENT (1902-1994)

First Stage: Trust versus Mistrust (Infant): As an infant, I would assume that my needs were met by my mother; however, being that I cannot remember this time of my life, all I can do is assume. I do believe that during this stage of development mistrust was where I fell into. I am still to this day "apprehensive and suspicious around people" (Boeree 2006).

Second Stage: Autonomy versus Shame and Doubt (Toddler): Looking back into my childhood, I would have to make assumptions, yet again, at this stage. During this stage, when I was around two years old, I had developed double pneumonia. I was told by my older half brother that I had crawled off the side of the porch during a storm and laid in the rain for hours, "exploration or developing my independence" (Boeree 2006). I was in the hospital for some time, and I was unable to hold down any type of food. The last hope was being fed intravenously through my head, and my mother was told that this would be the last attempt. I was read my last rites. This I would assume was severe neglect by my parents. I am a very compulsive person, as I must try to do everything right, so I would say that I developed this compulsiveness at this stage.

Third Stage: Initiative versus Guilt (Preschooler): This stage, in my opinion, is where my foundation as an adult was found. Being that I was not watched over and that I was afforded the opportunity to be creative, I developed a strong sense of independence, and I knew I had to fend for myself; however I never reached the point where I was merciless.

Fourth Stage: Industry versus Inferiority (School-Age Child): During this stage a teacher, a guidance counselor, and the mother of one of the very few friends that I had, helped me find balance between latency and industry.

Fifth Stage: Identity versus Role Confusion (Adolescent): This stage of development proves to be a very dangerous time of discovery; this stage of development could have ended terribly with me either dead or imprisoned. Being that I was born and raised within the inner city of Clairton, a small community known for drugs and other illegal activities, and the peer pressure that did exist, along with my low self-esteem and aggressive behavior, my life could have ended. However, being that I had a strong resolve to find love due to the lack of love my entire young life, I realized that this life of crime was not conducive to my dreams. I did have a problem with identity. I played every sport possible, I worked many little jobs throughout the neighborhood, and I associated myself with a local drug dealer for a short span. Looking back on this time in my life, I can actually say this stage cemented my resolve to become more than what most expected of me, and that expectation that people held was that I would one day be imprisoned or found dead on the streets.

Sixth Stage: Intimacy versus Isolation (Young Adult): I have always wanted a loving relationship for as long as I can remember. I believe that this is because of the lack of positive loving relationships during my life span throughout my adolescent years. I have been married now for twenty-five years, and our relationship is truly wonderful. During this stage, I knew what I wanted in my life, a loving relationship, a career to provide for a future family, and security in all aspects of my life; however, alcoholism was holding me back at this time, and I was in complete denial. I did have a discovery of self later in this stage.

Sobriety and a better understanding of self were the key components. I then moved on to the next stage.

Seventh Stage: Generativity versus Self-absorption (Middle-Age Adult): This is the stage that I am at now, as is my wife. We have an outreach program, and we just finished a walk called "The March for the Next Generation." This march was dynamic in that the purpose was multifaceted. Not only did I do this march to the White House, which we marched one-hundred-eighty miles, for the inequalities that exist within the inner cities, but I did this for self-discovery. This march identified me as being sincere in my quest and proved to society that I was resolved and had purpose of life.

Eighth Stage: Older Adult (Integrity versus Despair): Although I have not yet entered this stage yet, I can see signs of entering. I do find myself reflecting on my accomplishments, as I do enter the thoughts of my death. At this point in my life, death is not a concern; I am not afraid to die. My attitude about death is unique in that my life purpose was to serve God and that upon death, this should be a joyous occasion. I feel a deep passion toward my religious beliefs, and I feel thisk is or should be a part of everyone's life. I do realize that many people live a wholesome life, morally and ethically sound without a religious belief; this is an accepted choice, and I honor and respect this decision. Having God in my life was a personal choice and has brought my much comfort, so death to me is a part of life, and I have been working very hard to serve God. And the ultimate goal is to sit in the kingdom of heaven.

My growth or personal development throughout my life span was based mostly on negative experiences; however because of these negative experiences, I learned to welcome growth, to aspire, and to dream. I wanted to achieve more than people thought I ever would. I wanted to become a productive, compassionate, and loving individual within my society, and I have.

Viewing my personal growth, according to Kohlberg's stages of moral development

I. Preconventional

Stage 1: The Punishment and Obedience Orientation

This stage was a confusing time of life. Being that abuse was taking place every day and in many different forms, distinguishing between righteous punishment and wrongful punishment was unclear. Although I tried to avoid punishment, most times, I could not. I became isolated and avoided contact with any human being. The positive growth at this stage came in a development of imagination, creativity, and inner strength.

Stage 2: The Instrumental-Relativist Orientation

During this stage of my moral development, I transgressed in the sense of human compassion. I avoided any kind of relationships out of shame and embarrassment. I did not have the opportunity to give in any capacity to another human being. During this stage, my aggression revealed itself. I began getting into fistfights on a regular basis, and in many cases, I was hardly provoked. I developed a reputation as being antisocial. In a sense, I did satisfy my needs at this time of development; however, these needs were not morally sound.

II. Conventional Level

Stage 3: The Interpersonal Concordance or Orientation

Early in this stage, whether someone approved or disapproved of my successes or failures was meaningless. However, during this time, certain individuals in my life, my teacher, guidance counselor, and a friend's mother, helped me develop to a certain degree; and with this, my life began to change for the better, not much. I truly began to accept the stereotypical response to my aggression and to some degree relished in this attitude; this provided me the opportunity to climb back into my shell when I desired. My solitude provided me the opportunity to grow, meaning, I believe this to be the stage where my future plans were developed, being everything my family or home environment was not.

Stage 4: The "Law and Order" Orientation

During this stage, I entered into the U.S. Marine Corps. This provided me the growth needed to adjust to social order. Also, this is where doing one's duty was a necessity and/or expected in order to succeed. I also learned respect; we had a saying in the marines that I remember to this day: "Discipline is the instant obedience to orders and self-respect." I live by these words to this day. This is where my sense of being morally sound began to emerge.

III. POSTCONVENTIONAL

Stage 5: Social Contract

I established many traits while serving in the Marine Corps. And during this time, I met my wife of twenty-five years, who was a devout Catholic. This combination of Marine Corps beliefs and principles, along with developing a strong belief in God, enabled my personal values to finally be developed. I began to understand the importance of relationships and how developing compassion and love helped in my personal development. This was the most important milestone in my life.

Stage 6: The Universal-Ethical-Principles Orientation

This is the stage of development of morality and ethics in which I am currently at. I believe that my experiences through each stage of Kohlberg's moral development and that of Erikson's stages of development met at this juncture of my life. My moral and ethical growth were slow to develop; however, this merger took place because of specific points throughout my life, such as Mrs. Albert, the guidance counselor, the Marine Corps, my wife, and through her I incorporated a strong religious belief system. These milestones brought to my current self and were the reasons for my success, pertaining to my choice of attending graduate school, my passion for life, and my compassion for society as a whole.

My attitude toward gender differences was developed from early childhood. My mother was the only source of positive growth, but this attention only came when my father was not present, so suffice it to say, her attention was sporadic and was not constant. During my educational experience in grade school, again, the positive attention that I received was from women—Mrs. Albert and Mrs. Geletko, my guidance counselor. My wife demonstrated a softness and passion that I have never experienced before, and with these women throughout my life, I gained a great appreciation toward women as a whole.

Being that I had endured the race wars within our city (this happened during the civil rights movement) and that my ancestry in the United States did not date back to the days of slavery, my parents harbored no prejudice toward African-Americans. On the contrary, they were disgusted by the unfair treatment and the inequalities that truly did exist during this time. The environment that I grew up in was predominantly African-American, and I was raised to accept people for who they are. The color of their skin was irrelevant. I still hold on to this positive life lesson that I learned throughout my life span.

As can be seen throughout this life span, Mr. Hodish's moral and ethical growth developed equally as compared to Erikson's stages of growth. The environment that Mr. Hodish was raised in and his attitude toward gender and cultural influences coincided precisely at the same time of Erikson's stages of development and that of Kohlberg's stages of moral growth. The experiences that Mr. Hodish experienced throughout his life were what propelled him on his present course—that of being a productive human being who is genuinely concerned with societal norms, a man who holds no negativity toward gender differences, and a man who does not distinguish or judge others because of their race or culture.

The following comparison chart will demonstrate the relationship between Kohlberg's stages of moral development and that of Erikson's stages of development. The chart will also exemplify the growth from infant to older adult and will demonstrate the moral growth of John Hodish at each stage of his life. The highlighted words in the chart were designed to show the commonalities at each stage of development and how Mr. Hodish's moral and ethical growth was formed throughout his life span.

Comparison Chart

AGE OF DEVELOPMENT	ERIKSON'S STAGES OF DEVELOPMENT	KOHLBERG'S STAGES OF MORAL DEVELOPMENT	COMBINED DEVELOPMENTAL OUTCOME
Infant/Toddler	*First Stage: Apprehension and suspicion around people Second Stage:* **Independence** *and compulsiveness*	*First Stage of Moral Development, Outcome: First Stage:* **Imagination, creativity**, *and inner strength.*	**Creativity and imagination, independence** *and compulsiveness.*
Preschooler/ School-Age Child	*Third Stage:* **Independence** *Fourth Stage: Balance between latency and industry*	*Second Stage: Aggressive and* **antisocial**	**Independent, antisocial**, *balance between latency and industry.*
Adolescent	*Fifth Stage:* **Low self-esteem and aggressive behavior**	*Third Stage:* **Aggressive and solitary**	**Aggressive and solitary, with low self-esteem**
Young Adult	*Sixth Stage:* **Discovery of self, understanding of self**	*Fourth Stage:* **Adjustment to social order, self-respect, discipline, obedience, moral and ethical growth**	**Self-growth, discipline, obedience, moral and ethical growth**
Middle-Aged Adult	*Seventh Stage: Sincerity,* **self-discovery**, *resolve, purpose of life*	*Fifth Stage: Compassion,* **personal development**	**Development of self**
Older Adult	*Eighth Stage:* **God**	*Sixth Stage:* **Moral and ethical growth, passion and compassion**	**God, morals and ethics, passion, and compassion**

The formation of self is our identity. A unique individual and our collection of memories of past experiences and events will signify the emergence of who we are. The self will develop and emerge.

In this individual example, the key component to altering perception was the discovery of self. And to further this, when we can reach the point in our life that we begin to care and think about someone other than ourselves, then and only then will we experience true freedom; we will escape from the mental shackles that enslave us in a personal darkness. Being able to extend ourselves toward others and helping them to go beyond the mental self-imposed boundaries will only strengthen the community bond that is desperately needed within the inner cities; this will also help promote positive self-growth and mental health. This belief lends itself to psychodynamic or intrapsychic Psychology, which was developed by Freud and his students in the early 1900s. This belief is stated by Mauriello (2010), as "human behavior to be a result of unconscious, innate needs, drives, motives, and patterns. These forces dictate a belief that our outer behavior is a direct result of our deep-seated inner processes resulting from our personal and collective past."

Another area that is stunting the growth of inner-city dwellers, specifically adolescents, is cultural. The irony being that we live in such a culturally diverse society, but the inner-city dwellers are not exposed to the wonderful contributions that every culture has put forth. This ignorance brings contempt, and if all were exposed to the cultural contributions that were made by each subcultural living within our society, all would be aware that beauty in each culture does exist and not all members of a certain subculture are deviant. Over the past three years, the author of this document has been rather productive in behavior modification at the CCOP. His strong resolve in that mixed cultural experiences, the arts, would bring certain adhesiveness among each inner city, as well as the suburbs, has been proven to be effective. John Hodish, the director of affairs of the CCOP, has implemented many programs that are conducive to establishing a certain community pride, as well as bridging the gap between the inner city and those who live on the outskirts of the inner city. At the CCOP, amateur boxing is one such program that builds discipline, self-esteem, honor, and integrity. This program also demonstrates the importance of sportsmanship, being that there will be times that we will lose, but the important issue is how we handle this. The message being sent to the participants involved in this program is the way we accept defeat; rising up and continuing our on our path is more important than winning. Another program at the outreach center is the art club. Currently, we are involved in a mural that will be painted on the side of the building. We will let the participants paint an area of the building that is expressly their own creation. We believe that allowing this expression will relieve much stress and that each participant will be able to take pride in this meaningful endeavor; expression lasts a lifetime. We also offer a gospel choir, being that we are Christian-based. This choir will have the opportunity to take stage throughout the city of Pittsburgh, exposing each participant of the choir to a new environment. We also have an improvisational drama club. This group of adolescents will have topics that they will act out, unscripted, and a few of the topics that we will present to society are issues that are plaguing our inner cities. Some of the topics will be teen pregnancies, gangbanging, and alcohol and substance abuse. These plays will afford a glimpse into the minds of our young and will allow audience participation at the end of each play; confronting the players of the drama club with questions will also afford valuable insight into the mind-set of our young.

These three programs will unite as one show, a Christmas show specifically, where the choir will perform, and then a Christmas play will follow, and the art club will create the wardrobe and background. This event will be held within the community of Clairton, and the logic behind this is to unite the community as a whole and to celebrate a new beginning within the inner city.

We at the CCOP also offer spiritual counseling, as well as individual and family counseling for those who are affected by alcohol and substance abuse, use, and/or addiction. We have a varied approach to treatment for alcohol and substance abuse. Being that we are a Christian-based program center, treatment programs that revolve around a religious belief system can be implemented. Also, we believe that the holistic and/or the eclectic approach to treatment are effective, and we encourage all participants who enter our facility to participate in one of the cultural programs that we have. Reducing stress and being able to relax in a safe environment are conducive toward recovery from many of the presenting problems within the inner city. Our services offer clients a mental and physical state of wellness. We approach our clientele with a holistic approach to their recovery whether the presenting problem is a behavioral or mental disorder. We also approach those who are suffering from alcohol or other drug (AOD) use, abuse, and/or addiction using the biopsychosocial model and/or the eclectic model for those who may be presenting a co-occurring behavior for assessment. We approach those who are suffering from AOD using the Minnesota Model for recovery.

Our program is multifaceted when treating those who are in need of behavioral modification. Whether this modification is due in part to AOD or their behavior is eclectic, we offer alternatives toward recovery. Our program is based primarily on individual growth and physical and mental wellness, and we achieve these positive goals with a stringent program of physical fitness, community service, and lastly individual services toward self-discovery.

Our clientele will measure their intestinal fortitude every day in order to achieve self-worth, and this personal growth is guaranteed. We have a specialized training program that is second to none, and we offer the individuals the opportunity to examine their desire and need to grow physically and mentally beyond the negative path of self-destruction through this program; we will demonstrate the effects of the mind-body connection through hard physical training and mental awareness. We also demonstrate to our clients the importance of having a strong sense of community social skills, knowing the reliant nature of community and family is relevant toward recovery either from behavior issues or AOD.

Our program also offers to those who are seeking recovery from AOD the needed resources to attain this goal. We offer informal individual counseling, family counseling, and spiritual counseling; and we help aid in this process through self-examination by exposing this particular clientele to the mind-body connection as well.

To simplify this document in terms of order, meaning, what steps are needed to combat deviant behavior and to modify the behavior of those who are suffering from behavioral disorders will now be presented.

The Therapeutic Process:
Altering Perceptions: Inner-City Gangs

Knowing the formation of the perceptions that each (each is in regard to the singular mind set of the group mentality) is the first key concept that a counselor should know. This is the most important aspect—researching the subculture—thoroughly, within any inner city throughout our society. Entering into a counseling practice within the inner city with only a preview of what this community is will not produce positive results and may in fact cause more harm than good. The forthright posture of these individuals, gangbangers, and even the community as a whole will be more than startling for those who are not familiar with this kind of destructive lifestyle. Also, upon the initial meeting with a resident or gangbanger, these individuals will take a defensive posture as well: they will not be willing to open up an honest dialogue until trust is established. An expressed explanation as to the client's rights, specifically confidentiality, should take the entire first session. Documentation and, if possible and allowed by the client, video footage of the sessions should be taken. This should be explained to the client that this footage will never be seen, only in the case of the client harming his or herself or when the threat of harm or death is placed on anyone by the client or an associate of the client; this meaning that if the client would threaten to harm or kill the counselor or any of the counselors associates. This footage will be evidence of this. This initial understanding between the counselor and the client has to be expressed in a serious manner, and the counselor has to present this with a hard stance. Being that counselors within the inner cities throughout our society will be living in different states, adhering to the code of ethics within this state is a must. Also, with any legal issues that may arise during sessions, an attorney would need to be consulted; an explanation to the client of all the team members who will be associated with the case should be expressed in the first session also. And lastly, after trust and understanding (a friendship is imminent) has been established, any visual cues of gang affiliations must not be present in the counselor's place of business.

The Psychoanalytic and the Family Systems Thinking Model: The Inner City

The Psychodynamic Approach:

In this case study of inner-city dwellers, the psychoanalytic approach as well as the family systems model will be used. The logic behind using the psychodynamic approach and the family systems thinking is that within the inner city, there are many variables that can be detrimental toward health and wellness. The deviant behavior that exists within the inner cities stem from single parenthood, drug and alcohol abuse, use, and/or addiction, gangbangers and a very high crime rate, to name a few. Also, the inequalities that exist is devastating these communities, such as employment and education. This is where the psychoanalytic model will be used. The group mentality within the inner cities that is a phenomenon that has been in existence for quite some time. A target date, historically, could be since the civil rights movement. Today, this group mentality is acceptant of mediocrity and complacency, and the community is also acceptant of much of the deviance that does exist. As an example, drug trafficking is accepted by many in that this is a way of support for families. With this drug trafficking, the issue of territory arises, hence the gang wars that exist today to protect their environment. This is where the use of the family systems model will be used.

The similarities that exist between these two models, the psychodynamic and the family systems model, are few, but one such similarity is what will bond these two theories together—that being the individual mentality of each unique resident or deviant and how this unique individual mind-set is in essence the formation of a family mind-set. The difference between these two models is obvious. One focuses on the individuality, the psychodynamic model, and the family systems is focused on the group mentality and adjusting alternatives and resources to benefit the individual. The adjustment of integrating these two is not necessary; however, how these models overlap is the key. Using the psychodynamic model upon assessment, and through counseling, once the counseling team reaches the point of termination of therapy, the individual will be presented options or pathways to choose from that will further their identity and cultural and educational growth. This effort will be to adjust these perspectives so as to ultimately demonstrate to each unique individual their self-worth and how they can be productive citizens—the alleviation of deviant behavior.

THE COUNSELOR'S ROLE IN PSYCHODYNAMIC THERAPY

The counselor's role in psychodynamic therapy is to maintain a sense of neutrality. As stated by Corey (2009), "The analysts engage in very little self-disclosure and maintain a sense of neutrality to foster a transference relationship in which their clients will make projections onto them" (p. 69). The analyst will also try and surface the unconsciousness, to bring the unconscious conscious. Bringing about the unconsciousness to the level of consciousness is significant in that the counselor is striving to have the client relive these earlier experiences that were repressed in order to work through these hidden memories. In due course, the therapist or counselor wants to succeed in bringing emotional and intellectual awareness to the client. Also, as Gerald Corey (2009) states, "Strengthening the ego so that behavior is based more on reality and less on instinctual cravings or irrational guilt" is also another goal of the therapist or counselor (p. 69). And lastly, the goal of the therapist or counselor is working through the unresolved developmental stages.

The intervention strategies used in the psychodynamic approach are, as stated by Corey (2009), "free association, dream analysis, analysis and interpretation of transference, and analysis and interpretation of resistance" (pp. 75-77). These intervention strategies support the concepts and philosophy of the theory in that they are designed to reach the unconscious memory and to surface or bring to the conscious level; with these memories, the feelings associated with these hidden thoughts will be revealed and analyzed and interpreted for the client. Also, as stated by Corey (2009), "There is more frequent use of supportive interventions—such as reassurance, expressions of empathy and support, and suggestions—and more self-disclosure by the therapist" (p. 74).

An added intervention that is used at the CCOP is evolving a life span development plan for each client. Many, if not all, of the residents within the inner city of Clairton has witnessed traumatic events, such as murder or serious bodily injury to another human being or watching friends or family members suffer because of drug and alcohol use whether through individual use or through the criminal behavior due to these addictions. These traumatic events are deep-seated and usually are not forthcoming from the client so when devising the life span development plan, this has to be done at the pace set by the client. The counselor or therapist should not place much emphasis on this procedure, taking a casual posture would be required, meaning that if the client senses that the counselor is probing too deeply, they will have a tendency to take a defensive posture. As a counselor or therapist, maintaining a sound ethical practice would be required to disclose any procedures that are going to take place during the counseling sessions. This is an instance where refraining from telling the client of this procedure should wait until the life span development plan is finished; however, the counselor or therapist could possibly detect in their client if they would be willing to share in this endeavor. A judgment can be made for each client as to whether or not disclosure of this procedure should be done before or after the completion of the life span development plan.

As with any intervention within the psychodynamic therapeutic method, interpretation will follow. While in the Freudian perspective, the analyzing should be done by the therapist or counselor, if the therapist or counselor develops a healthy working relationship with the client, considerations as to having an open dialogue with the client pertaining to certain events within the life span of the client may prove to be effective. This is an alternative given within the CCOP.

The cultural limitations are that the psychodynamic approach is costly, and this form of treatment was established on the values of those from the upper—or middle-class communities of our society. Also, the cultural dilemma could be present in that some cultures may not appreciate this approach. This approach can be ambiguous for some. For example, and as stated by Corey (2009), "many Asian-American clients may prefer a more structured, problem-oriented approach to counseling and may not continue therapy if a nondirective approach is employed" (p. 87).

Another area of concern is that finding a trained psychoanalyst can be trying, and for those who come from a low socioeconomic society, this also will present a problem. Not only would this type of therapy be costly, but for many from the low socioeconomic community, their needs, such as housing, food, and the basic struggles that life in the financial depressed communities offer, is outside of the value of this form of treatment; however, this is not to say that these individuals would not find value in this form of treatment after their basic needs are met.

There is a long-time commitment using the psychodynamic approach, and this can pose a problem also. Many individuals are not willing to put a great amount of time into the recovery process. The attainment of their therapeutic goals are expected as quickly as possible.

THE FAMILY SYSTEMS THINKING MODEL:
(REFER TO THE SECTION ON EXPLANATION OF DEVIANT BEHAVIOR)

The family systems model has been spoken of in depth throughout this manuscript, specifically the community resilience theory. Integrating the community resilience model with the psychoanalytic approach will serve well within the inner city. The mind-set is outside of the norms of society and the many variables that come into play when speaking of the health and wellness of the inner-city dwellers. Having an enriched view of the client's mind-set and past experiences will necessitate the need for this type of therapy. Many of the residents within the inner cities have witnessed rape, murder, and many other traumatic events, and with using the psychodynamic approach, the exploration of the unconscious will be made available. The mind-set of the vast community can be compared to one who would be suffering from Stockholm Syndrome. Being that the gangs (which in essence are the same as terrorists) are in fact holding the resident's hostage, over the years, the inner-city community has grown to understand and, in many cases, accept this deviant behavior as a way of life. As stated by Katina Krasnec (2004), "The Stockholm Syndrome has been invoked to describe the results of slavery upon the African-Americans psyche, abusive relationships between men and women, or any situations where the division of power within a relationship or any kind is severely unequal" (p. 2). This is an intriguing concept of the Stockholm Syndrome in that Krasnec refers to the times of slavery and how the psyche of the African-Americans may have acquired this syndrome. This statement invokes the consideration that this may be a generational mind-set—this cognitive response being ingrained in the minds of the slaves and handed down throughout the years. Another interesting facet of the Stockholm Syndrome and the most influential in law enforcement circles, explained in the *Journal of Police Crisis Negotiations* based upon the Freudian theory, written by Ian K. McKenzie (2004), states, "[S]trentz (1979), a key figure in the Behavioral Science Unit of the FBI at that time, suggested that the syndrome is an 'automatic, probably unconscious response to the trauma of becoming a victim.' This approach suggests that because of a severe psychological threat, the ego defends itself in a number of different ways. One of the vehicles of defense is to 'identify with the aggressor.' Such identification requires that the individual takes on the beliefs, values, and behaviors of a source of threat and by so doing removes them as a threat."

The variables that allow Stockholm syndrome to develop is when the imprisoned individual or victim (resident) perceives the threat of death being imminent if he or she does not oblige the captor (gangbanger) and the reality that the hostage taker has the means to carry out this threat. This perception is a reality within any inner city that has gangs. The resident within the inner cities cannot run or hide from the aggressor because in most cases, the resident does not have the means to do so. And to act on one's own, referring to contacting the police, snitching, this will provoke the aggressor toward violence. In essence, the resident is isolated and the only means of survival is to comply with the aggressor.

An intriguing approach by the aggressor, whether this display is sincere or a thought-out act of deception, is to demonstrate some small portion of compassion within the community. Many times, the staff has witnessed a known deviant spending his own drug money on families that may be having a hard time feeding their children, and then the next day, seeing one of the family members who had accepted this act of kindness being beat or murdered. An incident had occurred in Clairton, Pennsylvania in the year of 2009 when a young man, his name being withheld, age sixteen, a member of the gang ABM, murdered his eighty-two-year-old female neighbor. This event occurred when this young man, who would do this elderly woman favors, such as cutting her grass, refused to let him take her car. He did not have a license to begin with. This young man, in a fit of rage, stomped this woman in the head repeatedly and then slit her throat. In essence, the resident within the inner city feels compelled to indulge these gangbangers and to be completely compliant. And in many cases, residents are happy to have escaped the notice of the gangbangers roaming the streets. The slanted cognitive process of this syndrome serves a function, and this is where the distorted relationship begins. The main concept of the community resilience theory, as a whole, is that the power will shift from the gangbanger to the community.

While the family systems model will be used as a building process for the client, the community itself will undergo recovery. The community resilience theory (Hodish 2009) will have a resounding effect that will free this imprisoned mentality throughout the inner city of Clairton. This recovery approach will take three to five years, and being certain that a relapse will occur on occasion, perseverance will ultimately win out.

How the community resilience project will be implemented will be to unite the churches, family centers, the educational system, and the municipality as a whole. Having community seminars once a month to present expectations and desired goals that the community itself will be responsible for.

The expectations of the establishments will be to extend themselves into the community, meaning, they have to make their presence known in a loving and caring way. When certain residents are acting inappropriately, the establishment owner, and this is depending on the situation, will either contact the police immediately or, if the business owner feels confident, will negotiate this deviance on his or her own. Also, the residents themselves will be expected to do the same. The logic behind this approach is to squeeze the deviants into the shadows, and eventually, the deviance will be known, no longer hidden behind a hood and a bandana. The community needs to take back the streets. Support groups will be necessary, and a constant vigilance is required.

The necessity for support groups throughout a community that is implementing a plan such as the one this manuscript is offering is essential for recovery; not only for the deviants but for the community as well. The psychodynamic approach is recommended due to the deep-seated traumatic experiences of the inner-city dwellers. As was stated, some of the neurosis could stem from the slavery days, and the symptoms of this syndrome may have been passed down through the generations. This may be argumentative. However, using the psychodynamic approach still holds value in that this recovery process may need much time to take effect and the traumatic events that many have witnessed within the inner cities may have placed certain memories at the unconscious level.

Postures and Attitudes of the Therapeutic Session

The Counselor:

Visual cues are very important from the client. A firm handshake, always looking the client in the eyes, is necessary. If the client offers a smile, return one accordingly, meaning, if the client expresses him or herself in a grand way, this should be reciprocated. If the client presents no smile, you should only present a quick smile. The counselor really needs to have an understanding of the common quirks that are present within their practicing community. Being joyful and happy when someone is in a depressive state of mind can be insulting. This is the mind-set of many, specifically within the inner city. Do not be surprised if at some point the client will become angry, and using the smile as an example, the client may respond to this casual smile by saying, "What the fuck you think is so funny?" The most important part of counseling within the inner city is empathy, but not to the point where this empathy may appear as a weakness on the counselor's part. There is a phrase that many people in the streets of the hood use, this being, "Don't mistake my kindness for weakness." Never appear weak or soft-hearted with a client from an inner city. Also, active listening is crucial as their way of speaking will differ from the norms of the vast society due in most part of this culture, not because of a lack of education. This is the inner-city identity, and visual cues, signs, dress, and talk are unique in each and every inner city.

By no means should the client ever feel disrespected. This could cause the client to leave the counseling session, and in some cases, this may trigger a verbal assault and possibly a physical one as well, depending on the level of disrespect. In essence, always be honest but respectful.

Always be honest and to the point. Being aware of the client's educational level, speaking in terms that he or she will understand, is necessary. Educational inequalities within the inner cities are real; and as stated by Natriello and Pallas (1990), "achievement scores are strongly linked to school racial composition and so is the presence of highly qualified and experienced teachers" (p. 5), and that, as stated by Balfanz and Legter (2001), "the nation's shockingly high dropout problem is squarely concentrated in heavily minority high schools in big cities" (p. 5). And finally, Orfield and Lee (2005), state, "[T]he high level of poverty among children, together with many housing policies and practices which exclude poor people from most communities, means that students in inner-city schools face isolation not only from the white community but also from middle class schools. Minority children are far more likely than whites to grow up in persistent poverty" (p. 1).

By no means should a counselor barter or accept gifts for counseling services. If the client cannot afford the rates of your practice, offer the client free sessions, lower your rates, or refer the client. After the therapeutic relationship has blossomed to a friendship, if a small gift is offered, refusing this gift would be considered an insult. Accept this small gift with a thank-you, and do not question the motive behind this gift. Once the relationship is sound, the client may ask for rides to or from their residence or at times to take them to job interviews or various other places. The counselor has to be wary of this for various reasons. The first reason is the safety of the counselor. Going into some places within the inner city can be very dangerous. Secondly, this practice can become an expectation on the client's part; once this is started, refusing can cost the therapeutic relationship. This is a very touchy area, and each case will be different. The best way to handle this is to say no. Ethically extending the friendship beyond the confines of the office would be considered unethical.

Never lend or offer the client money. If the client asks, kindly say no, that this will strain the client-counselor relationship. This will occur so be prepared. If you lend money to a client, chances are you will not get it back, and this will become an expectation that the client will hold. He or she will ask again, and when you respond no, a confrontation may occur. If you offer money, this may be an insult to some; pride is in essence the only thing many inner-city dwellers can call their own.

The common characteristic of any inner-city resident will hold specific characteristics. The initial posture will usually be one of mistrust of the counselor and his or her associates, and reluctance of participation in this initial assessment will undoubtedly be present. There will also be an air of defiance and defensiveness present within the client. The client may present a certain level of hostility and may appear at times to be somewhat aggressive. These barriers to effective counseling will dissipate after some time, and this will be dependent on the counselors approach as to how long this negative posture of the client will remain.

The Posture and Approach of the Counselor:

1. Always be respectful.
2. Always present active listening.
3. Always be forthright and honest.
4. Never lose control of the counseling session. Stay within the framework of your therapeutic approach.
5. Always demonstrate empathy.

THE CARETAKER:

The parent of an adolescent who may be in a gang, or this adolescent while not in a gang, may exhibit a certain level of deviant behavior, will present anxiety, depression, and/or anger. In some cases, comorbidity will be present. The parent—or this should be stated as the caretaker because, in many cases, relatives raise the child—will have a genuine concern and will actively participate in counseling; however the counselor has to remain in control. Stay within the framework of your applied therapeutic approach, do not deviate, and always remain respectful at all times.

The caretaker will initially be intolerant, and the role of the counselor will have to be to explain to the caretaker that the case may take some time. At this initial assessment, actively listen. Look for visual cues as this may provide insight into the caretaker's personal life. What this means is that many individuals within the inner city may be drinking alcohol or partaking in illegal substances. Look for the clues. Many residents within the inner city suffer from domestic abuse, and many inner-city residents have educational levels not at the national standard. Both the visual cues, as well as body language, are a vital part of the therapeutic process.

Initially, the client will not be forthright about his or her personal life, and this may take one or two sessions before this client will offer the truth as to whether he or she is participating in any behavior outside of the norm of the vast majority of our society.

The initial assessment is crucial as this will determine whether or not this client will come back. Remain focused during this first session. Let the client speak freely. Encouragement and support are necessary, as is empathy.

Another issue that the counselor should be aware of is that many women today are single-parenting. This, single parenting brings about many detrimental variables that lead to the child deviant behavior. And while the intentions of this single parent may be honorable, the single mother has so many responsibilities to handle that the child may get lost in the hectic pace of the mother. This is another factor as to why certain individuals may join gangs, or in the least, reaches out to other deviants, regardless of a gang affiliation. As stated by Warren Ballentine (2010):

> [C]hildren of unmarried mothers of any race are more likely to perform poorly in school, go to prison, use drugs, be poor as adults, and have their own children out of wedlock. The black community's 72 percent rate eclipses that of most other groups: 17 percent of Asians, 29 percent of whites, 53 percent of Hispanics and 66 percent of Native Americans were born to unwed mothers in 2008, the most recent year for which government figures are available. The rate for the overall U.S. population was 41 percent.

This is a startling statistic that has to be realized by all those who are providing counseling to an inner-city deviant or family. Understanding the strife of the single mother, empathizing with her, and sincerely listening will begin the process of building a positive relationship. Also, if the counselor is a man, trust will be an issue in most cases. The male counselor will also have to establish trust; do not indicate any form of attraction or actions that may be construed as an attraction. Obviously, and we should know if we are in the counseling field, forming a relationship in a way that can be construed as sexual or even an attraction other than a professional one would be considered unethical. Check the state code of ethics.

Being that so many of the single parents are young, we at the CCOP provide classes on parenting skills. The members for this particular class have not been well received by the community. We are now making an effort to circulate advertisement for this particular class, and we are considering involving the local magistrate to court-order teenage mothers who are demonstrating deviant behavior to attend our parenting class.

The Posture and Approach of the Counselor:

1. Be understanding.
2. Show empathy.
3. Listen actively.

4. When necessary, be forthright.
5. Always demonstrate respect.
6. Be inspirational.

THE DEVIANT:

Before the counseling session begins with a gangbanger or a deviant from an inner city, make sure that the culture is well understood and has been researched extensively. Being able to recognize the gangs dress, colors, some signing with their hands, and their speech will aid immensely in effective counseling.

A few examples of how to recognize gang affiliations verbally and visually would be:

Deviant 1. Melissa's party is gonna be jumpin', **homies.**

The word "homies" is a respectful response to the dead gangbangers from their hood. The word "homies" is associated with the gang ABM (All 'Bout Money) in Clairton, Pennsylvania. Their colors are blue.

Deviant 2. Melissa's party is gonna be jumpin', **cracks.**

The word "cracks' is characteristic of the city Duquesne Pennsylvania. While this city has no gang affiliations, they ride as a city. Their colors are black.

These were just two small examples of how a counselor can identify gang affiliations. Knowing the characteristics and/or the level of criminal activities that this gang participates in will also determine the seriousness of the intervention of a particular client. For instance, if this gang has a high rate of murder convictions, it is likely that the only way a gangbanger will be allowed to separate from this gang would be through death. If he leaves, they will kill him or her. Or if the gang has a very low murder rate or none at all, the chances of an individual leaving this gang could be by jumping out. This meaning that the individual will have to endure a group beating by the gang. This beating can last five or ten minutes and can leave permanent damage to the individual. Knowing the gang affiliation and the intricacies of this gang will increase the chances of effective counseling. Kristina Hutch Matthews (1997), in "An Interview with Lisa Taylor-Austin," spent seven years counseling gang members ("gang-bangers") in the city of Los Angeles. When asked what motivates kids to join, Lisa Taylor-Austin (1997) states:

[I] think that most people want to get jumped into a gang because they're interested in finding a place where they can feel like they belong. They're looking for love, respect, a bond that they'll have with other people. For the larger gangs, once you've jumped in, you're in for life. The only way out is to die out.

This phenomenon that exists, gangs, and the ritualistic attributes, have to be understood as a way of life—a reality that exists, a common characteristic that, as an example, Catholics celebrate Christmas, gangs have meaningful rituals also that they hold sacred, and these rituals span the entire United States throughout every inner city. This specific personality has to be understood that many of these gangbangers were born into this life style, and trying to coerce am alternate lifestyle would be futile by a single counselor or therapist. This does not suggest that an effort should not be made on the contrary; hence, the logic of the author of this manuscript that if one can be saved, it was all worthwhile.

The deviant during counseling will be reluctant to participate; in many cases, this individual will be court-ordered to attend counseling services. If the counselor is attending to a court-ordered client, the counselor's approach will be much different from when attending to a deviant seeking help. Let us begin with the court-ordered deviant.

The court-ordered deviant will be defiant and will have the perspective that the counselor is full of shit and knows nothing of life on the streets. This is when the counselor, if in fact is from the inner city, knows the streets and the rules of the street should firmly state his or her street resume, meaning, that the counselor should enlighten this client of all that he or she did do when on the streets, whether the counselor was in a gang, drank alcohol, sold drugs, gangbanged, etc. The goal of the street-smart counselor will take the role of the "old head." This term is a street term, and what this term suggests is that the old head knows the tricks of the trade, has experienced life in the streets, is wise, and carries a certain level of respect. In essence, the street smart counselor is no longer seeking the role of counselor per se; the counselor is seeking the role of the old head. This is very important for the counselor to understand, and he or she can make the difference in counseling a deviant such as this.

This particular deviant will be borderline sinister, will be forthright, and at times may present a physical threat, do not show weakness; however, always be respectful. When you as the counselor feel the need to speak something that may be borderline disrespectful, make the point to say no disrespect meant.

Building a trusting relationship, let alone a friendly one, with this client will take at least three to four weeks. Do not get into a habit of trying to buy his or her loyalty; if they ask for something trivial, say no, and do not hesitate to say no. If you see that they may be in need of an item, let's say, a toothbrush or hairbrush (this happens often in placement shelters), buy them one. This will go a long way in establishing a relationship. If you would like, buy them a snack or even something from a fast-food establishment. Never let them know where you live or never take them to your home.

When I was working as a front-line counselor at a local placement shelter, I would always bring in a bag of double cheeseburgers from McDonald's once a week. I would also buy personal items for some of the residents, usually those who did not have family members who could afford to do so or who did not care. I also brought a few into my home. I did this because I was perceived as an old head, and many of the gangbangers let it be known that if anything would ever happen to me or my family, there would be serious repercussions. This sentiment was held by many different gang members, and while this was a huge chance on my part, this was effective. The logic behind this plan of action was to demonstrate a commonality among rival gang members, that love can be shared across imaginary territorial boundaries, and that while I was from a different hood, a claimed old head from this specific hood, my love was afforded to all. This was stressed every day, and was well received. This approach is very dangerous and is not recommended for anyone. My success was mine, my methods were tailor-made for me. Do not try this method as this method can be very costly. Being creative is important, and learning a system that works for the individual counselor using all the therapeutic approaches is recommended. Below is a standard guideline for the counselor who is taking on this specific clientele.

The Posture and Approach of the Counselor

1. Be stern and forthright.
2. Always be respectful.
3. Never show weakness.
4. Do not be timid.
5. Be honest always.
6. Relate to this client, be understanding and caring.
7. Actively listen as they will tell you with complete honesty their problems.
8. Do not be offended by the use of foul language.

9. Do not get into a position as to succumbing to their needs; buying items of need randomly is okay, but do not buy them cigarettes and alcohol and never give them money.
10. Always be aware and alert.
11. Always be mindful of counter-transference.

The gangbanger who is seeking help, who is not court-ordered, can be managed as any other client, with one exception, a very serious one. This client will need alternatives, and while it is not customary for the counselor to give specific alternatives, this should be considered on a case-to-case basis. We have to be mindful that when a gangbanger seeks help, it is because of the realization that he or she is doing wrong, that they no longer desire the lifestyle of an active gang member. This individual realizes the consequences of trying to leave the gang lifestyle, and he or she is truly coming to you, the counselor or therapist for alternatives, for exit routes out of this lifestyle that will be veiled with security' they know they can possibly die because of this present action.

An example of this would be during the summer of 2009 at the CCOP, a nongangbanger was who had just recently moved to the city of Clairton, Pennsylvania, frequented the CCOP. I immediately took a liking to this young man, age nineteen, and developed a friendship with him. The building of this relationship did not take long, just a matter of weeks, and within this time I discovered certain truths of this young man. One of these truths was that he was not living with immediate family, his blood relatives were from Georgia. Secondly, he was selling drugs, crack to be specific, and lastly, he was using the outreach program as a safe haven. He knows that no one would ever do any harm to him while in my facility.

The major concern was that many times he would come into the facility beat up, and while he never snitched on anyone, which is a big mistake within the inner cities, he did not have to. Enough information was gathered to know what was going on. This young man was cutting into the known drug dealer's territory, and it was just a matter of time before this young man would be found dead.

The last time I saw this young man was when he ran into my facility, which fortunately I was their late, around nine thirty EST. If it was not opened, he may have been found dead. He stated that some certain individuals were trying to kill him, he exposed a handgun to me and said he will protect himself if need be. I told him he would soon be found dead, that he needs to go back to Georgia with his blood relatives if this was possible, he said it was. I drove this young man back to where he was staying, and never saw him sense.

There will be people who question this determination that I made, and I can understand why if this person who was confused as to why I handled this the way that I did was not from the inner city. The option of going to the police was not possible for many reasons, and while there will be many law enforcement officials out there who will argue this, they would be wrong. Going to the police in this instance would provoke the local gangbangers into a strong distrust, and truthfully speaking, I could not specifically finger any certain member so the entire gang would have been harassed. If this were to occur, knowing that I do have some juice (street term for "power") with these gangbangers, my reputation would have taken a serious blow and my effectiveness with dealing with the cities gang would be extinguished; thus, criminal activity would again be on the rise. Taking this young man out of harm's way demonstrated not only to the city gang that I will do what is necessary to protect life, which validated my sincerity to the cause and strengthened my relationship with these deviants throughout the city. This action also demonstrated to the city officials that if need be, I will make judgment calls. This is a precarious place that I am in, in a sense. I could be considered harboring a criminal, but then again, I saved a life and protected the city from much gang-related criminal activity. Again, this is not an approach for everyone. My situation is unique, and I have been involved with the community of Clairton my whole life, I am known and respected. This is not the recommended course of action for anyone but me. This is a unique approach, do not do this.

The Posture and Approach of the Counselor:

1. Be attentive; apply active listening.
2. Be understanding and seek alternatives.
3. Establish a sense of urgency. Move slowly but effectively, and prioritize the necessity of this individual seeking change. His life may be in danger, or at the least possible physical harm may be forthcoming. If this individual has family members and this client feels retaliation coming toward his family, seeking the help of the police may be necessary; but this option would have to be discussed with the client unless death of any involved is possible. Trying to persuade the proper authorities is necessary at this point, and while being respectful at all times, be forthright and stand strong in your convictions.

Conclusion

Interestingly, when this manuscript began some years ago, I hypothesized that society would ignore my plea for help. Let me explain this a bit more in depth. I hypothesized that inner cities were in a state of complacency. This self-contentment is based on the generational mind-set of the inner-city dweller that what they have achieved is good enough—having a roof over their head, government funding to help their cost of living, and a poor school district. That standard of education is not anywhere close to equivalent suburban standards. This mediocrity is acceptable, this is enough.

Many inner-city dwellers were nurtured into this mind-set, through hate crimes against blacks, Hispanics, and those of Asian descent, these communities were to stay put, don't cause any commotion, and be happy they were lucky to get what they you got, this elusive promised freedom. White America and those minorities who have stepped beyond the invisible racial barriers, look down on inner-city dwellers even to this day. The inner-city dweller was and still is considered to be a frightening community that is less than equal. They will never be nothing more than what they are today—a stigma on society.

The CCOP was initially created as a research facility, meaning, I wanted to implement a program center to help the mental state of the inner city. I wanted to demonstrate that we, the inner-city dwellers, can rise above the expectations of how white America has viewed us. In the past, racism, prejudices, and biases were the invisible shackles that kept inner-city dwellers enslaved. And while there are still many people who still hold these prejudices and biases toward minorities, the perspective of many has shifted—racism, prejudices, and biases still exist, always will, but the shift from minorities, not completely, has been directed to poor people in general.

When the CCOP began its journey in the year 2008 (this is when we were a legitimate nonprofit organization), we, meaning that me and Mr. Geletko, a friend of fifteen years or so and a partner in the organization of the CCOP, decided to march from Clairton, Pennsylvania, to Washington, District of Columbia, the White House, to raise awareness and of course money for our program center. Our beginning point of walk was in front of our program center, which I might point out, no one showed up for our farewell except for family members, the volunteers from our program center, and one or two others; no city officials were there. The march was roughly two hundred miles or so, and this took us five days to walk. We carried with us water supplies that fit snugly into a small backpack which also carried essentials, such as extra clothes, snacks, ibuprofen, and other items, which made our backpacks roughly thirty-five pounds. We also had in our backpacks a big envelope that held our business plan, grant information, and a plaque for President Obama, to whom we were hoping to give them to when we reached our final destination, the White House. We were interviewed by four newspapers and one radio talk show. We estimated that over fourteen thousand subscribers were reached.

Throughout our march, Tristan and I speculated about how much money we would raise. We both agreed that we would probably receive none, but we dreamt what we would do with the money if we did receive any at all; we received not a penny, the only thing we received was really big blisters and very sore backs. But on the positive side, my hypothesis was proven true.

The CCOP actually started as a PAL Boxing Club, with the representative of PAL appointing me the director of affairs. I was greatly appreciative of the PAL organization, and I embraced this opportunity with all my might. The boxing program alone was not bringing in enough people however, and as a major contributor for the boxing club, the name will be withheld suggested offering more programs, which in actuality prompted the birth of the CCOP. The implementation of the programs was put in place, and we began to grow; we had thirty to fifty individuals every day.

The lease holder on this building was the PAL representative, and he was to pay one dollar a year for ten years, and his contractual obligation was to pay the utilities, do general upkeep of the facility, fix the leaking roof, and to hold one boxing show a year for the duration of the contractual agreement. The lease holder did not live up to his end of this contractual agreement so the city of Clairton officials locked the doors for good. My wife, Ruth Ann, went to the program center to open one day in January of 2011, as it was her day to lead the art club, and there were ten to fifteen young children waiting with smiles on their faces. When my wife went to open the door, she realized that we were locked out. When she came home, she was livid, explained what had happened so I went immediately to the municipal building for answers. Naturally they explained the reasoning behind the locked the doors, stating insurance reasons and the fact that the PAL representative did not live up to the contractual obligations; I understood.

The city officials did state that my community relations, as well as our programs were of great appreciation, and they led me to believe that when this PAL representative was off the lease agreement. I would be placed on the lease; I was ecstatic. After a few months of going back and forth with the city officials, I was offered by the city manager and one of the council members the opportunity to buy this building. While I was a bit perplexed as to why I was not being put on the lease agreement and instead being forced to buy this building, they must have sensed my disapproval and stated that they could not just give me a building, that other residents would be upset by this, and stated, just give us a figure. I gave the offer of five thousand dollars, and they said yes. One week after this acceptance, I went back to the city to discuss a few details and was told by the city manager that they were no longer offering me the building; rather, they were going to place this building on the open market, and the starting bid was going to be my offer of five thousand dollars, I was aghast by this unethical display by professionals, and I stated this.

Needless to say, my efforts have been thwarted, and we, the CCOP are homeless. We are currently planning a weekend in August of 2011 to hold a revival and a boxing show for the residents in the city of Clairton, free of course. Our efforts now have been compromised, and we had to rearrange our efforts from serving our residents completely, to serving them minimally while trying to raise money for another facility.

The deep-seated mentality of those within the inner city is based on mediocrity and complacency. Trying to break this thought process is very hard, especially when those who are in power are more concerned about personal agendas rather than the health and wellness of those they are to serve. I hope and pray that all those who have read this book have gained a greater understanding as to the plight of all those who are dwelling within the inner cities throughout our country.

The generational mind-set of the inner-city dwellers is an obstacle that produces barriers toward positive change. Try as we may, this mind-set breeds contempt and distrust toward anyone who does not match a certain criteria set forth by this group mentality. An example of this is, being that I am Caucasian, and although I was born and raised within this particular inner city of Clairton, Pennsylvania, some feel, meaning, certain African-Americans, that a white man could not possibly counsel black children. This harsh statement has a tendency to nurture an ongoing distrust of not only me, who many consider a wonderful man and some feel that is one who is reestablishing the civil rights movement. Just imagine how many feel about a white counselor who has no intimacy with any inner city. Failure is imminent.

As was stated throughout this manuscript, this mind-set is not only of the African-American communities but is a shared mind-set throughout our society, pointedly of any inner city that is financially distraught. This phenomenon is startling, scary, and very real. The brutality that can exist within the mean streets of the inner cities can never be described; this can only be lived. And through this tumultuous existence of many inner-city deviants, this can mean but two things—death or prison.

Trying to change who we are without the knowledge of other meaningful existences can be compared to knowing there is a better way, but not knowing what this other way looks like, feels like, tastes like, and smells like. An innate sense of wrong may exist, but this feeling quickly vanishes when our children are crying because they are hungry. Or when one of our family members need medical assistance but does not have the money or transportation to receive this needed care. And the desire to provide in these examples is so overpowering that the alternative to provide a certain amount of relief spurns one to commit a heinous act out of survival. Can we really blame them or the system in which we live?

What is disheartening is that many can understand the necessity to commit some of the crimes that happen within the inner city. Robbery, burglary, and at times even murder are acceptable within this brick-and-mortar prison. Every act outside of the norms of our society is a cry out for help, but being the proud people that they are, those who live in this environment will never admit this. Fuck it, they say, and I have heard this too many times . . . but I understand, not condone.

To those who have read this book in its entirety, do not except blame for this lifestyle. Do not offer pity. You will not find this to be a good approach. Do not offer anything but sincerity in understanding. Try to minimize the unique personal dilemmas into small concentrations and manageable segments and arrange these problematic nuggets into an order of importance. This will allow you the counselor to unfold the inner self of the client as these nuggets of dilemmas unravel.

The catch phrase that we use at the CCOP is "creating life-defining moments for positive change." This is a very important concept because the only defining moments that are offered within any inner city are negative ones, for the most part. We as inner-city counselors or therapists have to step outside of our comfort zone, in that while the office counselor stays within the comforts of his or her own domain, which I am not trying to disregard this practice, but the inner-city counselor or therapist will not be as effective in a working environment such as this. This is an element where personal judgment on the counselor's part will come into play. Knowing the environment intimately and then extending oneself into the community is extremely effective but takes a certain kind of person to be able to do this. With the ability to extend beyond the office walls of one's practice will greatly enhance the effectiveness of one's practice and will allow a greater opportunity in the effort to create these life-defining moments for each client.

We as counselors within the inner city also have to face the ugly truth that we cannot save everyone, and more times than not, we will see more failures than successes. Although in a whole, as seen in the working model of the CCOP, we can make positive change for the community in helping one individual at a time. A case study will be presented now highlighting the effectiveness of creating defining moments.

CASE STUDY: THE ACCOUNTS OF SAMANTHA ANN GRIFFITH

Samantha, who we call Sammy, was born January 18, 1990, in Erie, Pennsylvania, at Saint Vincent Hospital. She was raised in an environment of despair. Her mother, who started using drugs and consuming alcohol eventually, became addicted when Sammy was around the age of five, during her preschool years. Sammy never knew her real father, but she did have a stepfather, who smoked marijuana and was abusive both verbally and physically. He would fondle Sammy when she was going through her school year stage of development up until her early adolescent years. He would also make sexually explicit jokes on a regular basis. Sammy's stepfather on the positive would offer some comfort on occasion through protecting her when her mother would become aggressive and hostile toward Sammy.

Sammy's mother would leave the house on occasion, and at times this abandonment would go for days at a time. She would plead with her mother to stay home, but this only spurned hostilities. Because of these times of abandonment, she decided to move in with her grandmother. Her grandmother was a positive role model; however this did not work out; Sammy, being so young, brought about too much stress and anxiety so her grandmother had to send her back home.

There was a brief intervention that Sammy found throughout her preschool years and into her adolescent years, and this was the Neighborhood Art House. This organization offered Sammy peace of mind, a place where she could escape the abuse that she endured on a daily basis, if only for a few hours a day. Also, at the time when she was five years old, there was a medical concern that was life-threatening, so much so that she became a Make A Wish recipient. Tumors were discovered in her stomach that she is still living with till this day; she did not have medical insurance her whole life up until the year of 2011. She is currently looking into the removal of these tumors.

She could not stay with her grandmother anymore. This placed her back with her mother and stepfather. An event that started the independence of Sammy, and demonstrated the inner-strength that she possessed, follows: One Easter, or somewhere close to this holiday, in the year of 2005, Sammy's mother had disappeared for days. Sammy would pray to God to help her. Sammy decided at the age of thirteen to call her case worker to come and take her from this abusive environment; the case worker did just that.

While in foster care, she had the opportunity to be taken in by an African-American woman who Sammy said was a racist and did not offer herself to her on a personal level. Sammy felt as if this woman really did not want to from a close relationship because this woman denied her any quality time in which Sammy so desperately needed. Also stated by Sammy, this woman was always belittling her, putting her down, as did her mother and stepfather. This arrangement did not last long, and Sammy soon found herself back in foster care.

Sammy stayed in this foster care system for a year and was finally offered by her cousins to come and stay with them. Sammy did just that for two years at the age of sixteen and seventeen. While living there, she stated that she was verbally attacked daily, that all they did was put her down. She was very uncomfortable living there, and soon after she turned seventeen, she decided to go out into the world on her own. She did.

While on her own, she got a job working in a warehouse, making roughly seven hundred dollars a month. She met a young man that she was attracted to, and a relationship blossomed. This relationship, unbeknownst to Sammy at this time, was going to be another life-defining moment. While Sammy stated this young man was less than she had hoped for, he did introduce her to the world of amateur boxing. She decided then, upon seeing this sport up close, that this is something she would like to do.

Sammy has stated that she always knew that one day she was going to be successful. She felt that her personal relationship with God was going to produce a lifestyle that she would be content with. She started her amateur boxing career in the town of Butler in Pennsylvania.

We, meaning, Philly and I, and our other trainer from the CCOP, Tristan Geletko, were at an amateur boxing sporting event with one of our elite amateur boxers, and at this time, we had never heard of Sammy in the boxing world. Our fighter who was fighting a young man out of Ohio, Pennsylvania, fought a beautiful fight. Although he lost, the outcome could have went either way, depending on who were the judges. Be it as it may, Sammy, who was in attendance watching this fight, immediately ran over to Philly after our fight and asked Philly if he would train her. Although Philly said yes, he was not sure how this was going to work out for a couple of reasons. First, this girl was being trained by another trainer, and second, while Sammy had displayed a lot of heart in her desire to come and train with Philly, she was poorly trained, and he did not know if he wanted to waste his or her time.

As it turned out, Philly took this young, beautiful, troubled young woman under his wing, as we do with all of our fighters, and began training her. Our concept at the CCOP is of a nurturing one. Philly and I are one of the same mind-set in that we ask no one for anything, and we expect nothing in return for our services. We help the young and old who are in need because that is our desire to do so for God or, from Philly's perspective, for Allah.

Philly took this Sammy into his home. He fed her and took care of her basic needs, and the process began. He gave her excellent training. I personally spent little time with Sammy because of my hectic schedule. I was working forty hours a week, attending college, working toward my MS in general mental health counseling, and being the CEO at our outreach program. However, Philly and I spoke daily of Sammy's development not only in her pursuit of a boxing career but her development of self.

Sammy, through the guidance of Philly, is now on track. She has a family that loves her. This would be me and my immediate family, Philly, and the CCOP in general. Sammy has a very good job now working for a huge hospital in the city of Pittsburgh as a nurse's aide. She has hospitalization now and is beginning the process of getting those tumors removed. And through her job, she will be attending nursing school at the University of Pittsburgh. Sammy's boxing career has skyrocketed; she is currently ranked fifth in the nation. Because of one positive life-defining moment, her path has been altered, thanks to Philly, and the greater effort by Sammy has undoubtedly changed this young woman from a life of uncertainty to a life of wonderful opportunities.

In summary of this book, we have found through a successful working model that not only can we alter the perceptions of an individual to be a productive moral and ethical individual who has the capacity to dream big and reach for the stars, but we can create this same mind-set for an entire community. The struggles in establishing a facility such as this is tremendous, and unless an individual has a full resolve and passion for an endeavor such as this, he or she will surely fail.

The barriers that exist at the onset of establishing a clone of the model presented in this book will initially be breaking down some racial and prejudicial biases that exist not only from the community that you are trying to save but from surrounding communities that have that will most assuredly have an agenda to see this model fail. This, meaning, the drug trafficking that is permeated from outside sources, the racial discrimination that will definitely exist, and the cowardly display of local politicians who hold their own personal agendas.

Please keep in mind that one person who has the determination and the compassion to succeed will. This is the first step. Secondly, interacting with the community residents, learning them intimately, establishing trust, and finally approaching the community municipality with a petition of the people, signed with their address and then notarized, will greatly enhance your chances of success. Asking the municipality to join you in a collaborative effort may also prove beneficial in that they may have an abandoned building that they will let you use.

This book covered in an entirety the formation of the inner city, the generational mind-set, the alterations of perceptions theory, as well as many other supporting theories. Counseling techniques, as well as posture and attitudes of all involved in a counseling session, have also been explored. And while there is so much more to be learned, the foundation of health and wellness has been explained and proven through a working model, the CCOP.

References

Balfanz, R. and Legter, N. (2001). *How many central city high schools have a severe dropout problem, where are they located, and who attends them?* Paper presented at Dropouts in America Conference, Cambridge, MA.

Bernard J. Baars, Stan Franklin (2003), *CONSCIOUSNESS IS COMPUTATIONAL: THE LIDA MODEL OF GLOBAL WORKSPACE THEORY*, Global Workspace Theory, acquired from http://www.theassc.org/files/assc/GWT-IJMC-2009.pdf

Bowlby J. (1953). *Child Care and the Growth of Love*. London: Penguin Books

Brookings Events, (2007) *What Makes A Terrorist, ANDERSON COURT REPORTING*, acquired from, http://www.brookings.edu/~/media/Files/ events/2007/0911terrorism/20070911.pdf

Brown v. Board of Education, *About the Case*, (2004), Brown Foundation for Educational Equity, Excellence and Research, acquired from http://brownvboard. org/summary/index.php

Carol Gilligan (1996) *Gilligan's In a Different Voice*, acquired from http://www.stolaf. edu/people/ huff/classes/handbook/Gilligan.html

Cloward, R. and Ohlin, L. (1960). *Delinquency and opportunity: A theory of delinquent gangs.* Glencoe, IL: Free Press.

Craig A. Anderson and Brad J. Bushman, (2002), *Human Aggression, Annual Review of Psychology,* Vol. 53: 27-51, DOI: 10.1146/annurev.psych.53.100901.135231

David Straker, (2004), Changing Minds.org, *Freud's Personality Factors, Three Levels of Awareness*, Retrieved From http://changingminds.org/ explanations/ personality/ freud_personality.htm

Robinson, Donald L., (1971), *Slavery and the Structure of American Politics*, 1765-1820. NY: Harcourt, Brace Jovanovich,).

Dr. C. George Boeree, (2007), *Personality Theories, SIGMUND FREUD (1856-1939)*, acquired from http://webspace.ship.edu/cgboer/freud.html

Erikson, E. H. (1963). Childhood and society. New York: W.W. Norton & Co., Inc.

Ezequiel Morsella, John A. Bargh, (2008), *The Unconscious Mind*, Abstract, doi: 10.1111/j.1745-6916.2008.00064.x, vol. 3 no. 1, 73-79.

Glasser, W. (1985). *Control theory: a new explanation of how we control our lives*. New York: Harper & Row. BF632.G551985X.

Gary Orfield and Chungmei Lee, (2005), *Why Segregation Matters: Poverty and Educational Inequality,* The Civil Rights Project, Harvard University, http:// www. civilrightsproject.harvard.edu

Gerald Corey, (2009), *Theory and Practice of Counseling and Psychotherapy*, [With CD Rom], Eighth Edition, Brooks/Cole, Cengage Learning

Greenwald AG, Klinger MR, Schuh ES., (1995), *Activation by marginally perceptible ("subliminal") stimuli: dissociation of unconscious from conscious cognition*, J Exp Psychol Gen. 1995 Mar;124(1):22-42, Department of Psychology NI-25, University of Washington, Seattle 98195, Retrieved December 6, 2010, from http://www.ncbi.nlm.nih.gov/pubmed/7897340?dopt=Citation

Guy Richard Mauriello, (2010), Solution-Focused Analysis: Psychotherapy For The 21st Century, *Excerpts on Empowerment and Life Purposes, Understanding the History of Psychology*, Acquired from http://www.psychotherapyfor.com/ archives/

archives/Harlan Beckley, *Facing Up To Inequalities*, from http://www.religion-online.org/showarticle.asp?title=2697

H. L. A. Hart, (1967), *Solidarity and the Enforcement of Morality,* acquired from http://64.233.169.132/search?q=cache:I4EipgxOxcJ:faculty.tcu.edu/rgalvin/readings/Social%2520Solidarity%2520 0and%2520the%2520Enforcement%2520of%2520Morality.doc+social+morality+codes&hl=en&ct=clnk&cd=7&gl=us&client=firefox-a

Herbert, Blumer, (1969), *Symbolic Interactionism, Perspective and Method*, Englewood Cliffs, NJ: Prentice-Hall Huitt, W., and Hummel, J. (2003). *Piaget's theory of cognitive development*. Educational Psychology Interactive, Valdosta, GA: Valdosta State University. Acquired December 5, 2010, from http://www.edpsycinteractive.org/ topics/cogsys/piaget.html

Jannica Heinström, (2003), "*Five personality dimensions and their influence on information Behavior*," Information Research, 9(1) paper 165 [Available at http://InformationR.net/ir/9-1/paper165.html]

Kail, Cavanaugh, (2008) *Developmental Psychology*, Executive Editors, Michele Baird, Maureen Straudt, Michael Stranz

Katina Krasnec, (2004), *Stockholm Syndrome: Unequal Power Relationships*, Acquired from http://serendip.brynmawr.edu/exchange/node/1896

Kristina Hutch Matthews, (2004), *An Interview with Lisa Taylor-Austin*, Next Step Magazine, Acquired from http://www.gangcolors.com/pdf/interview.pdf

Kohlberg, L. (1981). *Essays in moral development: The philosophy of moral development* (Vol. 1). San Francisco: Harper & Row.

Lala Mamedov, (2008), *Human Development*, KA 702, Overview Presentation, Slide 25, Retrieved from http://epistemist.com/Papers/Lev%20Vygotsky%20KA%20702%20Overview.ppt

Petee, (1987), Lecture 09—Social Psych, *Deviance*, Adapted from Sociology 530 paper; Handbook of Social Psychology; Handbook of Sociology, Retrieved April 21, 2009, From http://www.nd.edu/~rwilliam/xsoc530/deviance.html

Lindsey D. Nelson, (1998), Comm 3210: *Human Communication Theory*, University of Colorado at Boulder, acquired from http://www.colorado.edu/communication/meta-discourses/Papers/App_Papers/Nelson.htm

Craig Rains, (2000), Little Rock Central High 40th Anniversary, September, 1997—*The 40th Anniversary of One of America's Most Important Civil Rights Events,* 2000 Craig Rains /Public Relations, Inc., Retrieved from http://www.centralhigh57.org/

McCrae, R. R., and Costa, P. T., Jr. (in press). *Conceptions and correlates of Openness to Experience.* In S. R. Briggs, R. Hogan, and W. H. Jones (Eds.), Handbook of personality psychology. New York: Academic Press.

McKenzie, I. K. (2004). *The Stockholm Syndrome Revisited: Hostages, Relationships, Prediction, Control and Psychological Science.* Journal of Police Crisis Negotiations, 4(1), 5-21. doi:10.1300/J173v04n01_02

McLeod, S. A. (2007), *Simply Psychology* [On-line] UK: Available: http://www.simplypsychology.pwp.blueyonder.co.uk/ Accessed: March 22, 2011

MIA Library: Lev Vygotsky, *Lev Vygotsky Archive, 1896-1934,* acquired from http://www.marxists.org/archive/vygotsky/

Natriello, G., McDill, E. L., and Pallas, A. M. (1990). *Schooling disadvantaged children: Racing against catastrophe.* New York, NY: Teachers College Press; Schellenberg, S. (1999). Concentration of poverty Schellenberg, S. (1999). Concentration of poverty and the ongoing need for Title I. In G. Orfield and E.DeBray, (Eds.), *Hard Work for Good Schools(pp.130-146). Cambridge,* MA: The Civil Rights Project at Harvard University; Lee, C. (2004). *Racial segregation and educational outcomes in metropolitan Boston.* Cambridge: The Civil Rights Project at Harvard University.

Nikki M. Ruble, William L. Turner, (2000), A Systemic Analysis is of the Dynamics and Organization of Urban Street Gangs, *The American Journal of Family Therapy*, 28:117-132, Copyright ©2000 Brunner/Mazel, 0192-6187/00

Phil Ender, (1998), Education230A, *Introduction To Research Design And Statistics*, Preliminary Issues, external Validity, UCLA Department of Education, Acquired from http://www.gseis.ucla.edu/courses/ed230a2/internal.html

Piaget's Theory, *Continuous vs. Discontinuous*, Retrieved from http://psych.colorado.edu/~colunga/ p4684/piaget.pdf

Robert V. Kail, John C. Cavanaugh, (1992), *Human Development: A Life-Span View,*

Robert R. McCrae, Oliver P. John, (1991), *An Introduction to the Five-Factor Model, and Its Applications*, acquired from http://www.bsu.edu/web/00t0holtgrav/623/ ffmarticle.pdf

Robert Merton: *Anomie Theory*, Retrieved from http://www.d.umn.edu/ ~bmork/2306/ Theories/BAManomie.htm

Rutter, M. (1979). *Maternal deprivation*, 1972-1978: New findings, new concepts, new approaches. 283-305.

Servaas van der Berg, (2008), *education 10*, International Academy of Education, International Institute for Educational Planning, ISBN: 978-92-803-1322-2, Acquired by http://www.iiep.unesco.org/fileadmin/user_upload/Info_ Services_Publications/ pdf/2009/ EdPol10.pdf

Social Psychology, *Aggression,* acquired from http://www1.appstate.edu/~beckhp/ soclectureaggressionsq.htm

Sociological Theories To Explain Deviance, acquired From http://www.valdosta.edu/~klowney/devtheories.htm

Sutherland, Edwin H., and Van Vechten, C. C. Jr. (1934). *The reliability of criminal statistics.* Journal of criminal law and criminology, 25 (May-June): 10-20.

Stanford Encyclopedia Of Philosophy, Consciousness, First published Fri Jun 18, 2004; substantive revision Mon Aug 16, 2004, Robert Van Gulick, acquired from http:// plato.stanford.edu/entries/consciousness/

Strentz, T. (1979). *Law enforcement policy and the ego defenses of the hostage.* FBI Law Enforcement Bulletin, 48(1), 1-11.

Thomas L. Crandell, Corinne Haines Crandell, James W. Vander Zanden (2009), *Human Development*, Ninth Edition, McGraw-Hill: Mike Sugarman. Chapter 7 pg. 238-239, Chapter 9, pg. 309-310, Editor-in-Chief, Michael Ryan

Warren Ballentine, (2010), DISCUSSION: *72% Of Black Babies Are Born To Single Mothers—How Concerned Should We Be?* Acquired from http:// newstalkcleveland.com/national/warrenballentine/discussion-72-of-black-babies- are-born-to—single-mothers-how-concerned-should-we-be-video/

Wertsch, J. V., and Tulviste, P. (1992). L. S. Vygotsky and contemporary developmental psychology. *Developmental Psychology*, 28(4), 548-557. doi:10.1037/0012-1649.28.4.548

White, Jerry, (2000), World Socialist Web Site, wsws.org, *Former Klansmen indicted for murder in 1963bombing of Birmingham, Alabama church,* acquired from http://www.wsws.org/articles/2000/may2000/birm-m20.shtml

Zechmeister, J. S., Zechmeister, E. B., and Shaughness, J. J. (2001), *Essentials of Research methods in psychology.* Boston: McGraw-Hill

Index

M

Maternal Deprivation (Rutter), 29
Matthews, Kristina Hutch, 96
Mauriello, Guy Richard, 82
McCrae, Robert, 73
McKenzie, Ian K., 89
McLeod, S. A., 29, 116
Medlin, John Major, 11, 19-20, 109
Merton, Robert, 31
mind
  conscious, 54-55, 57, 87
  unconscious, 54-55, 57, 87
Morsella, Ezequiel, 54

N

Natriello, Gary, 92
naturalistic approach without intervention, 21
Neighborhood Art House, 108

O

Obama, Barack, 104
observation with intervention method, 21
Ohlin, Lloyd, 30
old heads, 49, 97-98
Orfield, Gary, 93

P

PAL Boxing Club, 104. See also CCOP (Clairton Community Outreach Program)
Pallas, Aaron, 92

perspective
  categories of, 56
  examples of factors to, 56-57
Philly. See Medlin, John Major
Piaget, Jean, 33-34, 55, 70
Positive Deviance, 63
poverty, 62, 64
psychodynamic approach, 16, 86, 87-89, 91

R

Ruble, Nikki M., 40-41
  Systemic Analysis of the Dynamics and Organization of Urban Street Gangs, A, 38
Rutter, Michael, 29
  Maternal Deprivation, 29

S

slavery, 24, 89
Stockholm syndrome, 15-16, 89
Stoudemire (reverend), 32
swagger, 30
Systemic Analysis of the Dynamics and Organization of Urban Street Gangs, A (Ruble and Turner), 38

T

Taylor-Austin, Lisa, 96, 115
terrorism, 61-62
theory
  alteration of perception, 53-54, 57, 59, 66-67
  anomie, 31, 117

CPSIA information can be obtained at www.ICGtesting.com
265306BV00001B/32/P

9 781462 870578